"Miller -- Read most of the book and a lot of it was interesting, but I can say that I wasn't very pleased with some things that were portrayed in the book-- some of your memories are not very accurate and are muddled by the 50 or 60 odd years that have passed. Some things that you have quoted me saying or printed are completely false or are a really large stretch, such as calling you a prick in the vacation school section-- I never used that word when I was 6 or 7 years old. Some of your language in the book is completely out of line. I would be embarrassed if my daughter or my grandchildren ever read it (by the way they never will if I can help it)-- When you write a book about family and friends you need to take into account the feelings of the people you are writing about before you put it into print. You printed some of things that are best left unsaid especially when family, children and friends are concerned or are going to read it. We all did a lot of things growing up that we aren't very proud of and surely wouldn't do again . It would be my suggestion to let the people you write about proof read the sections about them(if they are still alive) and have some input in what is being written. You can write an interesting essay or book without hurting anyone's feelings, embarrassing
them or the use foul language. If your sequels are going to be written in the same manner , I want you to leave me and my family completely out of them, comprende. Now, with all that being said, some of the chapters are interesting and the pictures are good. I wish you the best of luck in your endeavors. I know you and I had a great time growing up in Opp and have some great memories, but some of these memories are private and shouldn't be shared with our children. Please keep in mind what I have said because I'm very serious about that."

 . . . Testimonial from John R. Rue IV, Oct, 2007

Vacation Bible School Dropouts

Book ONE

Panky Miller

Greenbrae, CA

ISBN: 978-0-6151-6896-8

Library of Congress Control Number: 2007938659

Printed in the United States of America.

<u>Panky, Rego, and Butch, Opp, AL, circa 1950</u>

The Author with his first dog Jerry, Norfolk, VA

"Panky, why don't you write a book someday?"

"Hey, Miller, old boy. Tell us another one of your yarns 'bout the days when you lived in the Philippines, back durin' the '50's."

"Lordy pray tell, young man, you sho' can tell a tale. Why doesn't you put some of those crazy ideas in yo' head down on paper? Folks 'round here jus' might like to read 'bout you while you was growin' up durin' the summers down here, in Opp."

"Hank we've always thought you were crazy and now, with sixty five years of proof, we are totally convinced. How anyone has been able to get away with the things you have, and lived to tell about it is, in itself, nothing short of a miracle. Please share your insanity with others vis a vis the written word."

"Panky, do you suppose it's the Dean genes or simply the fact that being raised in that Navy family, traveling around the globe and never really settling down, always looking for a party, that has provided you with countless excuses for more bullshit to expound? I'd love to know the truth, if that were even remotely possible."

I was a horrible student in the developmental quadrant - probably read a total of five books during eight years of elementary academy. Then, college preparatory school at St Johns College demanded I become prolific in the procurement and the reading of <u>Classic Comics</u> which depicted, in summary and picture form, the entire length of the boring books assigned to us as homework. Suddenly, college arrived all too quickly and I was one lost plebeian in the numerous stacks filling the halls of the Auburn University Library, Alabama.

One summer, while working in Coronado, a predominately Navy town in southern California, I developed the urge to read, read, read. Suppose the primary reason for this newfound madness was that my compatriots, mostly Navy Juniors like me, were constantly dragging me into Perkins Book Worm, the local source for everything from Aristotle to Zorach, including Voltaire, Kafka, Clemens, Michener, Faulkner, Hugo and other authors' works that became my preoccupation while I endeavored to catch up on decades of lost time. Hence, I began a trend towards self-imposed literacy that would commence around the evening campfires on Coronado's North Beach while reading books recommended by my more enlightened peers. And, a catharsis ensued which resulted in this uncanny desire to write. Trouble is that it took me over thirty years to learn how to put pen to parchment.

My cousin, Rego, said that I should seriously consider writing a book that depicts the old country churches still standing in the rural deep South, juxtaposed with the last remaining honky-tonks close by. He seriously believes that both are entering a final chapter and that it would make for a good read and photojournalistic portrayal of our region. Saturday nights when Patsy Cline, Hank Williams, Webb Pierce, and many others would sing up a storm to be followed by quiet Sundays as folks spent their day around church services and family members asking the Almighty for forgiveness. That will be my next collaborative effort.

I acknowledge, first and foremost, my maternal grandparents, Birdie and Daddy Dean, whom I love and, in return, they taught me how to love the South. Then, I want to say how proud I am to have enjoyed five years of Baptist bliss at Auburn University where certain instructors hammered home the meaning of spirit, of being southern, of being creative, and technically correct when putting pen to paper. Next, a "Wheaties, Wheaties, Wheaties" hello and thanks to my former Navy wingmen in Attack Squadron 152 aboard USS Oriskany during the Viet Nam conflict. I consider you and your families as brothers and sisters, and we need another reunion soon, and not every decade, for heaven sakes.

Last but not least, thanks to my family who is chockablock with English majors, English journalists, English minors, English honor students, and authors. The die is cast. The legacy continues. Hell, I have nowhere to go but to my Macintosh computer for solitude. This newfangled contraption has everything-MacWrite, Word finder, Spell Checker, Correct Grammar, even a talking icon when I enter a misspelled word. Still, the creative portion is left entirely up to me. So, if it's crazy stuff you're looking for...

I acknowledge sixty five years of what some courts of law in this fine land of ours would describe as temporary insanity - not unlike the infamous defense used during Dan White's trial in San Francisco, during the late '70's, - after he assassinated the city mayor and a supervisor (albeit no assassinations on this side of the family).

Dan White's counsel pleaded the "Twinkie Defense" by scientifically deducing that the sugar contained in these delicious morsels caused a chemical imbalance and was largely the cause of White's temporary insanity, thereby leading him to shoot the mayor and supervisor while he was experiencing what we call a "sugar jag."

For various preposterous and unfounded reasons entirely devoid of Aristotelian logic, this writer has pleaded what is a first in the annals of jurisprudence. On the advice of those who are guarding my completely padded and highly secure future residence up at the California Veterans Home in Yountville, I have been strongly advised to cut through the deep voodoo and plead the "Boiled Peanut Dee-fense."

Can't you hear the bailiff now?

"Order in the court! Order in the court! You, in the rear of the room, quit spittin' those shells on the floor! Everyone please stand!"

"Your honor, may it please the court to know that we rest our entire case for the defendant, one Henry Louis Miller, Jr., alias Panky, on the fact that, as a young and innocent child, he consumed countless five cent bags of those boiled peanuts sold by a crazy man named Fireball, down in Opp, Alabama. The defendant's brain has been immersed in tons of that salty peanut brine for more almost seven decades, and this is why he fell off the deep end of surrealism and wrote a so-called anthology, titled Vacation Bible School Dropouts."

"Amen, brothers and sisters, have a good read!"

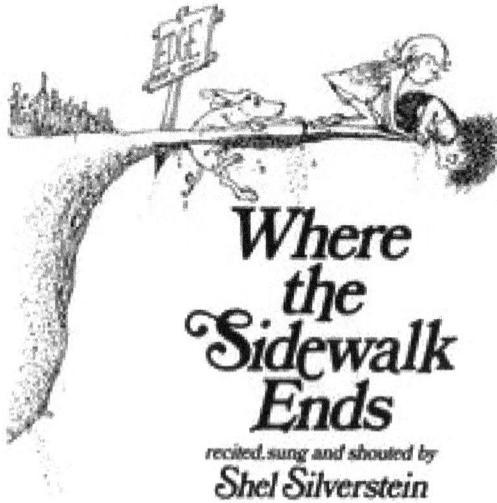

Where the Sidewalk Ends

recited, sung and shouted by
Shel Silverstein

Invitation !

If you are a dreamer, come in.

If you are a dreamer, a wisher, a liar,

A hope-er, a prayer, a magic bean buyer . .

If you're a pretender, come sit by the fire,

For we have some flax-golden tales to spin.

Come in!

Come in!

Sausalito, California

Daddy Dean's Drugstore, Opp, AL

The Sweet Shoppe

I am a southerner. I am from the Deep South and I can feel it right down to the kudzu between my toes. I can feel it in the pit of my stomach as the sour buttermilk oozes down my esophagus and curdles the cornbread awaiting its arrival. Outside, lightening bugs dot the night and become my beacons that signify the arrival of summer.

I am a southerner and my genes are saturated with the essence of those who inherit the soil and the sky and the swamps and bayous that comprise our geography and, of course, our soul. The red clay dirt permeates my skin and the sandy loam washes up from the Gulf to cover my paths. Southern oaks with the green moss clinging ever so gingerly between the scrawny branches fill my view around the lake. I know when the Magnolia are supposed to come into bloom save the harsh Winter that delays the process of Spring. The Dogwood sprinkles the rolling landscape bringing life to the otherwise homogeneously green pines. I am a southerner because I know these things and I anticipate the changes of the seasons where history records yet another passage, harvest, and the foliage expunging chlorophyll thus providing magnificent collages of leaves falling on the black asphalt byways and rutted dirt roads leading to wooden one-lane bridges, and to our farms. I am your county. I am your creeks and woods. I am your crossroads out in the middle of nowhere. I am your legacy to the town just over the ridge and down the country road past the turnoffs leading to somewhere. See those worn ruts down the sides of the mound left standing on that dirt road. The tires on my car fit perfectly as I careen towards somewhere but it seems like nowhere.

My ancestry can be traced back to President William Henry Harrison, Judge Barganier, who is Granny's adopted father, and the Dean family. Ancestral demons and demagogues and pimps and whores who roamed these places long before we descended from the north possess me. I can feel the spirit that inhabits all men of the south and invades their souls and spirits. This has been true for generations and the records are testimony of the accuracy of my hypothesis. Andrew Jackson, Thomas Jefferson, Harriet Beecher Stowe, Booker T. Washington, Robert E. Lee, Thomas Wolf, Jimmy Carter, W.T. Cash, Morris Dees, William Faulkner, Big Jim Folsom, Tennessee Williams, Flannery O'Conner, Robert Penn Warren and the list goes on and on to the point where redundancy is ostentatious and absurd. We write of desperation, corruption, anguish, prostration and abandonment. Southerners accept these characteristics and feelings as a way of life. We are able to mask the pain and exude a smile albeit a small one perhaps out of the corner of our mouth with a lip curled up indicating some sort of rancor.

I am of the same ilk and mettle of which nations are conceived. The Scottish, Irish, French and other western European civilizations dumped their bastards on our shores to purge their societies of purportedly useless illiterate peasants unworthy of assimilation into the cultured masses of Paris, Vienna, London, Stockholm and other evolving cities lying to our east. So be it. Folks back in the 1860's proposed two nations, one above and the other below the Mason-Dixon Line. Some southerners will never forget that war and the consequences resulting from abolition. Others, well it really doesn't matter because we are all slaves to this region, indentured forevermore to the unexplainable cosmos that captures and holds us to her bosom.

We are a visual people. Water towers depict where we are. I see the small dot on the horizon that signals my arrival in Opp. The bulbous gray monolith rises above the trees and low buildings and becomes the monument for high schools boys to utilize for significant rites of passage, such as hand-painted epithets. "Beat Kensington Eagles!" "Go Bobcats!" Beat those little peckerheads on the football gridiron, or my name painted here will be mud for another 365 days. Annual ritualistic misdemeanors, never enforced, surround the permanently embossed name of the town, followed by a comma, then the abbreviation of the state, like we don't really know where we are here in this county. a boldly painted OPP, AL alerts me to my pending arrival at Granny's. The juices in my body begin to flow more rapidly and my eyes widen with anxiety and anticipation of greeting family one more time. I am a southerner who cherishes friendships more than buckets of gold and ostentatious wealth. Kinfolk, fresh greens, scratch biscuits, raw buttermilk, and Mrs. Bird's lemon cake measure my pleasure. All right, I will concede and imbibe a wee bit of the 'Bama poteen, known as moonshine, when nights strikes and we meet at the Parkmore Drive In. I am a southerner.

*****

"This is one, monumentally sad, disastrous day in my life, Rue, and I'm not sure I can handle what I'm about to see. Years ago, you called and told me about it and how you felt as you drove up to the house. Now, twenty years later, I'm back to witness the biggest loss of my entire life, the reason I've been in counseling for the past five years. Ever had the wind knocked out of you? Ever had your nuts crushed on the cross bar of your bicycle? Or had some goober just plain kick the shit out of you until you wish you were dead? It's the same feeling knowing your true and blue sweetheart has been kissing some other guy, and you thought you were the first."

"Panky, you've got to get over it, boy. You'll feel the same way as I did and perhaps ever worse now that they are all gone but we have to get through this together. Butch is supposed to meet us at Delia's so we can walk the property and talk our way along and hug each other, but you kiss me and I'll knock your dick in the dirt, y'hear?"

"Rego, wait a minute. Who lived in this first house on the street? Remember we'd always stop and visit her first thing whenever I came down during the summers. She was a seam-stress, the sweetest little old lady in the world. She made all of the girl's dresses for the weddings and proms. As a matter of fact I think she made Virginia's dress for your senior prom. You know what really makes me sad, fucks me up royally? The fact these folks are all long gone, dead, in the ground. Most of them I only knew slightly and I never knew when they died and were buried. The only ones I knew were Dr. Waters, Mrs. Waters, and Harriet Cummins. Even old man Cole died when I was in Viet-nam. I helped to build his house that Christmas I worked in the freezing cold with those two old black men to unload all the bricks. So, here we are once again for more loss and pain. All I want to do is go on down to the Farmer's Restaurant, eat oysters, and drink some beer."

"Hush up. Here comes Butch up behind us. He knew all these folks his entire life so we have to be sensitive. This is his street just as much as it is ours."

"Hey Rego and Panky, sorry I'm late but then again I suppose you two are in no rush to get down to your granny's property. I'll pull over here and we'll walk down together."

East Ida Avenue is wide, with a landscaped boulevard strip down the center. Huge oak trees line the sidewalks on each side of the street. And, the colorful azaleas dot the center along with rhododendrons up and down the rows. Loamy sand spilling from the strip is scattered on top of the black asphalt.

There are about eight houses altogether on the entire street. Some have garage apartments in back but they aren't visible from the sidewalk. Did I say there were eight houses? Well, there are seven now. Granny and Daddy Dean's house burned to the ground sometime in the late 1980's and this is my first visit to Opp since then. Virginia Benton owned the house. She bought it from Mom and Aunt Evelyn when Granny died. Virginia turned it into a duplex rental. That really pissed me off. She had no right to tamper with this house. Rumor has it that it was struck by Jewish lightening one night and that was the end of that. I have tried several times to purchase the land from Virginia but she holds steadfast to an unreasonable figure for one, crummy empty lot that no one wants but me. Now, we have only memories of our childhood but there is still the playhouse in the back that was left unharmed. It is totally overgrown by vines and shrubs but you can barely see the roofline. Jesus, did we have a ball sleeping out there when we were growing up.

"Hey, Rego and Butch, let's go to the back and see if the bamboo grove is still standing. That's the same spot where Mom took our picture back in the fifties, the one I had blown up into posters for you two when I came back to visit in 1973."

"What do you know? Shit, here it is! Right next to the alley just as it was forty years ago. Ever heard of d'ej a vu? I'm having it now. Feels just like Gladdy Mae is going to run out the back door to tell us dinner's on the table. No hens cackling now. Miriam Donaldson's chicken coup is long gone. It was just behind the bamboo and you could really smell the chicken poop when it was hotter than hell outside."

"I've got my camera and tripod. Let me set it up and we'll re-invent that same shot of forty years ago. Even got black and white film for the occasion. Take of your shirts, stand right here, look at me and flex those fat arms. The timer will allow me to run over and stand next to you Rue. Here goes."

At Dean's Pharmacy

Lord God Almighty. So many changes but just look at this store, which appears to have been frozen in time. The marble counter is a wee bit duller, and there appears to be several more cracked tiles in the floor, but that's about the extent of any deterioration or change. Still plenty of faded Coke signs behind the marble counter. And several Atlantic malt machines line the back mirror ready for the onslaught of kids yelling for "More malt, more malt pleeeze!" The ceiling fans swirl and swirl round over our heads just out of reach so we can't threaten our little brothers by holding them up high and pretend that we're going to stick their heads in the path of the rotary blades.

Nonetheless, the luster has faded on those blades. And, the white floor tiles have yellowed with the hairline cracks winding their way through the isles. Big deal when you consider how many revolutions the fan blades have made over the past seventy-plus years of continuous operation, and everything else has a patina that only time and use provides. I can't imagine it any other way to tell you the truth.

Aside from the drugstore, a lot of businesses here on Main Street have a permanent "Gone fishin'" sign in the front window, for one reason or another. This place is beginning to resemble a ghost town. Lord God almighty! Can't the city fathers see that their single industry mentality is killing Opp? Most of the folks around here either work at the mill, or have businesses that supported its workers. And, every time some new entrepreneur tries to pursue interests in coming to Opp, our politicians make damn sure they don't get the building and other necessary permits. All this to protect the self-serving interests of a few fat cats at Opp-

Micolas Mills.

When was Opp in its heyday? I have a theory and it goes like this. I'm sure residents agree it was during the '50s. Every building in town was occupied and open for business. Opp had three drugstores, several clothing stores, hardware stores, mercantile economy stores, restaurants, jewelry stores, a thriving bus station, a hotel, a motel, two cotton gins, a theater, and a drive-in movie.

Then, a restaurant here in town suddenly closed down in the early sixties. Thus, began the decline and fall of Opp, as we know it today. Some of you may think I'm crazy, and you may be right, but my hypothesis is this:

"The rise and fall of Opp's prosperity is directly proportional to the rise and fall of The Sweet Shoppe."

Yes, brethren, I say before you that when Jim Sawyer went and killed hisself the ultimate demise of Opp's prosperity began, like that of Babylon and Rome, to crumble. And, no, I don't mean Rome, Georgia, which, by the way, had the best little whore house in the South. I surmise the correlation between the heyday of Opp, and the success of the Sweet Shoppe is when they boarded up that great little restaurant they began to board up this whole damn town! Now, if someone else has a better theory, let's hear it. Otherwise, I rest my case.

Berdie Bargarnier and Abner Dean while courting,

circa 1900

About the Characters

Birdie Barganier Dean, circa 1900

Know what Hank Williams, Aunt Ceil, and Birdie Barganier

Dean have in common?

First, I must assume that those who were either raised in the South, or simply love country and western music, are familiar with the greatest singer of all times. Hank Williams - songwriter, singer, vagabond, father, carouser, drunkard, strictly Alabama southern - has his guitar, his fancy boots with the rhinestones and various reptile skin appliqués, his oversized engraved silver belt buckles, his Stetson hats and his western-style cowboy suits, with the pointed pockets and pearly buttons, enshrined in the Alabama State Capitol Museum, for those of us who worship his music to view, forevermore.

Second, some folks are most likely asking, "Who in the hell cares what these people have in common? Never heard of the other two characters in my life." For further explanation, please continue.

Referring to a Rand McNally Road Atlas of the United States, locating the page outlining the great State of Alabama, the reader's eyes are drawn to the center of the state and the page where the capitol, Montgomery, is located. As the reader's eyes drift downwards to the southwest quadrant they will barely decipher one of the towns that does not warrant bold typeface or enlarged lettering because the population is less than fifteen to twenty thousand inhabitants. So, it becomes increasingly more difficult to locate because of the small size. Georgiana, is what one calls the roots, or the birthplace, or the childhood home, of the folks I just mentioned. When the state bureaucrats approved the funds to construct the great sprawling concrete horizontal tarmac, otherwise known as Interstate Highway 65, extending from Birmingham, down to Mobil, back in the late sixties, the engineers and planners bypassed many old hamlets, including Georgiana, so the once highly-traveled road for those driving from Montgomery, down to the Gulf coast, is now relegated to the locals, to the farmers, to the traveling salesmen who still rely on Georgiana, and other surrounding areas nearby for their livelihoods.

Used to be where travelers would see black men in the fields picking cotton, and the trucks parked outside the local cafe where the shop owners would congregate for coffee and the daily gossip. Never will forget driving through Georgiana, Monroeville, and other towns in the dead of winter, and seeing the older blacks huddled around the fifty-five gallon drums, with hot flames pouring forth, being used as make-shift fireplaces, to help take the freezing chill from the early morning air. Ain't supposed to get that in South Alabama, but it sho' nuff does.

In Georgiana, most of the townsfolk barely remember Hank Williams because he left as soon as he was old enough to sing and to earn his way while working in honkytonks around the state. However, the same is not true of one person who remained in Georgiana, for the greater part of her life. Aunt Ceil was one of the town matriarchs. And, an aunt she was not - only a title assumed by my ancestors. She is remembered as being one hundred and ten percent southern, and as being one hundred and ten percent dictatorial, territorial, and strict as hell.

Mr. and Mrs. Barganier lived and worked in Greenville, just a short piece down the road from Georgiana. Mrs. Barganier was a consummate teacher of music and she played the piano until the day she died. Mr. Barganier was a judge and a good one at that. Tough, but fair, was his reputation. Unfortunately, Mr. and Mrs. Barganier both died at early ages, leaving their daughter an orphan. But, for good fortune, a dear friend of the Barganiers, who lived down in Georgiana, assumed the responsibility of caring for and raising this young orphan.

Aunt Ceil was suddenly entrusted with the care of this baby in addition to three other small girls who resided in her household. This infant is known as Birdie, and Birdie Barganier was born in Greenville, on July Fifth, 1890. She passed away in Amory, Mississippi, in 1977 was laid to rest next to her husband of fifty-five years, Abner T. Dean, here in Opp. Between those two dates were countless episodes and memories that comprised her make-up, her personality, and her spirit that have lasting impressions on everyone she met because this is one person who, like others of her generation, had true grit. Her chemistry includes the stubbornness of the Scottish, the physical stamina of the Teutonics, the arrogance of the French, and the charisma of the Italians. This lady, Birdie Barganier, is my maternal grandmother.

For those of you who remember Birdie Bargainer Dean, otherwise known as Granny, she was a small person, in physical stature, about five feet plus an inch - basically a spit in the wind - who moved like a tornado through the streets and the dirt roads of Covington county. She followed the Baptist persuasion and she insisted that members of her family attend church services every Sunday morning. The only person who was exempt from this mandate was her husband. Lordy knows how he got away with missing services because the rest of the Dean clan, including "this Catholic", had to attend services even if it required driving twenty miles over to Andalusia in order to join the circuit priest for nine o'clock Mass.

Granny had absolutely no use for wimps. Right or wrong, she wanted you to stand tall and be heard, even if it resulted in her disagreeing with your convictions. Course, Granny'd never, and I mean never, tell you if she was dead wrong on a subject. Simply a thrust of her head in a sudden, upward manner, with a roll of her eyes, and a quick walk from the room would be the barometer of victory or defeat. And, that'd be the last you'd hear of it!

Granny's philosophy was, "Keep moving, do something worthwhile for the po' folks, and don't forget to say your prayers at bedtime." Sounds a lot like the philosophy stated in that best selling book, All You Really Need To Know You Learned in Kindergarten* Granny had simple tastes but she was very progressive for a woman raised in the deep South during her generation. I remember her introducing me to members of the only three Jewish families, in Opp. These families had suffered under the discrimination of so-called Christians, who professed brotherly love, and under the scrutiny of the Ku Klux Klan, whose members hated not only Jews but, in addition, Catholics and blacks. Granny recognized these three families, the Finkelsteins, the Muellers, and the Bukantzs, as God-fearing people who were stuck in a time and place trying to do their best just to survive in a small town. She taught me that these families and poor folks, like their more fortunate counterparts, have dignity too. Time and time again, Granny would reiterate that everyone, regardless of their color, religion, or income level, has pride, so they should be treated accordingly.

When I was home from Auburn one summer's day, she and I loaded up the old Chevy with some discarded clothes and linens, and we headed out towards the area of town near the hospital. I asked where we were going, and Granny said that we were donating these clothes and sundry items to a poor white family who lived up the road, apiece. Granny made me stay in the car as she walked up to the front door of this tar paper shack that was located across the highway from the Mizell Memorial County Hospital, on the back road to Red Hill. When the front door was opened and a figure appeared Granny merely handed the bags of clothes to the occupant, and she was back in the front seat within two or three minutes. She indicated where this was a family on the down and out, had a streak of bad luck, and needed some help for their children, but the family was too proud to ask for any assistance. Granny found out about the needs of these destitutes from Brother Hall, up at the First Baptist Church, and she set out on her task of collecting clothes and food, get the job done, and move on to the next daily activity without much dialogue.

Granny didn't stand there and dwell on the hardships of life or philosophize on the benevolence of good Christians but, instead, went on with her business fully cognizant that she wouldn't receive notoriety or compensation for her actions. Some force larger and more global would guide Granny throughout her life, and those of us who witnessed and experienced her actions, such as the donation to this poor family, never forgot them, and especially their significance. To this day, I am for the underdog, for the oppressed, for the poor, for the troubled masses, for Auburn whenever they play 'Bama."

For as long as I can remember Granny made me feel like someone special. My self-esteem soared whenever I reentered her sphere, and I'll never forget her visits with us in Bethesda, Corpus Christi, Washington, or Coronado, when, prior to her departure from Opp, Granny would load up a spare suitcase chock full with sugar cane just for me to peel, eat and suck the sugar straight from the stalk.

Soon after she arrived at our house I would ask, "Granny, let me help you with your bags. How long can you stay? Got enough luggage here for a month of Sundays. So good to see you, Granny, and I hope you never leave."

"Panky, you old, sweet thang, one of these bags is full of sugarcane, just for you. Now, don't go and eat it all the first day, or you'll be sick as a dawg!

As far back as I can remember Granny employed black maids. I prefer to call these maids nannies because not only did they cook and clean but, in addition, they watched over Rego and me as if we were their very own chillun'. The first nanny, who I can remember, was Ro Ceil who was very large, very, very black, sweet as could be, and dressed identical to the image portrayed on the Aunt Jemima Pancake box. I can still visualize her sitting on our back porch, under the shade of that white trellis, shelling field peas and cleaning sweet corn that she was preparing for the noontime dinner. Ro Ceil was full of spirit, proud and hard working.

When we drove Ro Ceil home in the mid afternoon she would get out of the car (always from the back seat) on the Montgomery highway, and walk over to her tarpaper shack situated near the city dump. The actual dump and saw mill adjacent to it were rather neutral in my mind's eye at that early age, but today the vision rings with depression, poverty, survival, disease, and every other negative aspect of segregation and deprivation so common in the rural South. Eventually, Ro Ceil and her family moved to the big city of Detroit, so her husband could secure better wages and, hopefully, work his way out of this downward spiral.

Following Ro Ceil was another maid named Gladdy Mae, who was Rego's and my perennial favorite. She reminded me of the slave's daughter Butterfly in Gone with the Wind. Gladdy Mae was small in physique but possessed a very large bosom for her petite size. And, her voice was rather high and squeaky, like that of a field mouse. But, let me tell you, she had Rego's and my numbers, and she knew that, if we misbehaved, one word to our mothers was all it would take for the switching hour to commence. That was the situation where Rego and I would be told, in no uncertain terms, to go into Granny's backyard, pick the greenest and most moist and flexible willow branches, return to the house, drop our freshly-starched, stiff-as-a-board Levi's, and then our BVD's, and bend over for several extremely painful blows to our hind legs and our butts! One of the most sever penalties we received for misbehavior, which included our being banned from the Royal Theater Saturday matinee double feature starring Whip Wilson, Lash Larue, Gene Autry, or Roy Rogers, "The King of the Cowboys," was because one day Gladdy Mae ratted to my mom and Aunt Evelyn. Reason being that Rego and I had referred to her physical endowments simply as her having big "titties." I cannot begin to tell you that hardened criminals down on the Atwood Prison Farm had an easier go of it than the two of us for this most heinous of crimes. Our legs and fannies were swollen for days, and our pride was hurt for weeks. When you missed a double feature at the Royal Theater matinee the news spread like wildfire among our peers. "Wonder what happened to Rego and Panky? Must have said something about Gladdy Mae's big titties again, or maybe they got caught chewing tobacco!" As the line in a popular southern movie released many years later would state, "Rego and Panky were simply having a bad day."

Everyone has rituals. Everyone has some sort of tradition that affects the moment; that affects the spirit, at the time, whether it is something as sophisticated as religion or voodoo or something as simple as clothing it is a colloquial statement of one's individualism and freedom. Rego and I had a colloquial statement and it went like this. We would buy the absolute tightest fitting Levis that could be buttoned around our waists. And, they had to be at least four inches too long in order to have the perfect two-inch double cuff. We're not through yet. In addition, our nanny was told, in no uncertain terms, that these Levis had to be starched so stiffly that they could literally stand up in the backyard by the tree that supported one end of the clothesline without any personal interference or assistance. When the Levis had dried Rego and I would slip into these ersatz cardboard stick figure cutouts, and a catharsis would ensue. Suddenly, we were as tough as those matinee idols we worshiped everyday, at two o'clock, right after we strapped on our two six shooters slung low around our skinny waists, with the holsters tied to our skinny legs. Watch out Roy, Dale, Trigger and Buttermilk, here we come!

Granny and Gladdy Mae never truly blended as employer-employee. I suppose that, both, possessed strong personalities that would not permit the other to get the upper hand, or to endure any criticism. Nonetheless, Gladdy Mae was a great friend, a great cook and we hope that she will have the opportunity to read this story one day.

Abner T. Dean, circa 1940

Where was A. T. Dean, Granny's spouse, when all of this chaos was occurring? Well, for the greater part of our childhood, he was busy running the store - Dean's Pharmacy. At one point in his career he owned every drugstore in Opp, which numbered six. During his career he eventually sold all but one and managed this store, until the late '40's, at which time he sold Dean's Pharmacy to old Charlie Williams, from down in Kinston, who ran the business for many years. Abner T. Dean became known as Daddy Dean to us.

Strange thing about southern folk and their colloquialisms and nicknames. Every boy with the Christian name of William, Stephen, Robert or Beauregard enlists an abbreviated title, such as Billy Bob, Bobbie, Bo, Stevie, Bubba, or another ridiculous macho concoction.

God only knows where his nickname originated but that was what we called Daddy Dean until he passed away in 1967 while I was in Vietnam and we still refer to him that way whenever we reminisce about those days. The only explanation for Daddy is none other than a simple abbreviation of granddaddy. Any other hypothesis would seem unlikely and unnecessary because, regardless of the reason, the South will always rely on these symbols of family traditions. Amazingly enough, one would think that, with the tremendous influx of families from northern and western states, these age-old habits would diminish. To the contrary, they seem to be self-perpetuating and a symbol of the southern heritage that will endure longer than the Appian Way leading out of ancient Rome, or the road to Sprayberry's Barbecue, up in Newnan, Georgia, just outside Atlanta.

My parents never told me about my family's roots. I suppose they didn't think I had the need know or was interested and that was a big mistake. I had to ask questions and listen to stories and facts spontaneously while attempting to accurately record items for future dissemination. One afternoon I was sitting on the bed and talking with Daddy Dean about my previous quarter at Auburn, and he began to tell me about his educational background and life prior to marrying Granny and moving down near Opp. I learned more about him during the next hour than I had during the previous twenty years. To hear Daddy Dean tell about his life was special, and I cannot even begin to convey the spirit with which he spoke in this writing. While all of the situations were either occurring or in the developmental stages, good old Daddy Dean was steadfast, hard working, and always up at his drugstore. He was the silent one, the rather intense one, who remained quiet and pensive. Daddy Dean wasn't a controversial person in that he preferred to play dominoes and to fish rather than discuss his political views. His origins were extremely southern, rural, and steeped in poverty. Born on a farm near Elba, AL he made his way over to the booming logging community, of Poley, which was situated on the outskirts of what was now his home of Opp. At that time, Poley, was the main community in this area and Opp, was in the rudimentary stages of evolving into a town. Daddy Dean found his way to the Poley store, which was referred to as the commissary, where he was given a job by the owner, a gent named Miller (no relation) who, also, owned the lumber mill. Miller soon realized that this hard working young man with great potential was virtually illiterate and, in order to retain him as an employee, he offered to provide Daddy Dean with free schooling, up in Montgomery, at the local business college. Daddy Dean accepted his kind offer and reported to school where he learned "The Three R's," and the basics of running a business.

Upon Daddy Dean's return to Poley, he was soon made the manager of the commissary and of the associated businesses at the Poley mill. Eventually, Daddy Dean had an opportunity to become an entrepreneur, thus began the start of his successful business career. He purchased the only pharmacy in the growing town of Opp, and Daddy Dean began to bring that fledgling business around to a profitable one. He hired registered pharmacists to handle the prescriptions while he took care of running the store. Soon thereafter, he purchased another pharmacy, which eventually led to his owning six pharmacies in this town of approximately six thousand denizens. Along with the acquisition of the pharmacies came the ownership of several buildings in town, which Daddy Dean leased, to other businessmen. And, then, one by one, he began to sell the pharmacies until there remained only one, Dean's Pharmacy, which still operates under the family name. As I said earlier, Charlie Williams purchased Dean's Pharmacy in the early 1950's and his widow, Charlotte, sold it to the present owner, Lloyd Sellers, in the early '70's. He recently sold it and retired n 2005.

Dean's Pharmacy is a landmark, in Opp. The store has an honest-to-god soda fountain, serving the only real Coca Colas formulated from carbonated water and patented syrup. The octagonal marble floors are original as are the porcelain-topped tables and drugstore chairs where we gather for morning and afternoon coffee breaks, and gossip. I must add that missing today are the china plates that held Delia Barganier's truly delicious homemade chicken salad sandwiches, with the white bread crust removed, wrapped in Cut-Rite wax paper - ten cents each - and the best you ever tasted!

I was told about Daddy Dean's death in a letter from my cousin, Stevie Rue, while serving aboard the USS Oriskany as a Naval Aviator, and it was worse than being shot down and taken prisoner in Hanoi. I felt like I had lost a portion of my spirit, my soul, my whole being. And I cried. I cried for hours as I slammed down a bottle of Grand Mariner, or Benedictine, or Black Jack. Can't remember the liquor label but I can remember that traumatic occasion vividly thirty years later.

I have an original photograph of Birdie and Abner while they were still courting, and my guess is that the photo was taken in 1911, one year prior to their marriage. This couple was glamorous in their Victorian attire - she in her long, white summer dress and he, wearing a suit, starched white shirt and his straw hat, typically referred to as a Boater. As a matter of fact, this may very well be the only photograph in existence portraying them in a candid pose. I personally don't believe either of them realized, at this time in their lives during the Great Depression that Abner would eventually become a very successful entrepreneur, and that Birdie would assist in the creation of two fine southern ladies, Evelyn and Lucille.

Panky Miller and Rego Rue, circa 1948

Now, there is a real duo who roamed all points of Covington county - Opp, Kinston, Andalusia, Florala, Lake Gant, Red Level, and the dirt, two-lane ultra-narrow country back roads that are simply just too numerous to mention. Evelyn and Lucy's finest, or so we thought. Anyway, we are the oldest which seems to be very significant when people ask about members of one's family. The middle aged kids get lost in the shuffle and the youngest always seem to get along in spite of being dealt a short hand on many occasions.

The two primary characters are blonde with hazel eyes. Panky was the skinniest kid who ever walked the earth. Rego was more athletically built taking after his father. Both were full of mischief and grew up only a few inches of escaping full fledged child abuse inflicted by their parents who would have been found innocent in any court of law once the judge witnessed the boys' behavior.

Lucille and Evelyn, circa 1974

Birdie Barganier Dean bore two daughters, Evelyn and Lucille. Aunt Evelyn and my mother, Lucy, were born and raised in Opp, where they resided at 309 East Ida Avenue, the same address where those of us who would follow resided, if only for a summer's vacation or a holiday. Evelyn and Lucille Dean were two lucky dames because not only were they very attractive but they were, also, blessed with aptitudes that would eventually provide them with a first rate education after high school. Both my aunt and my mother had propensities for music and that was a preferred career or hobby for southern belles so they, both, applied and were accepted by Huntington College, up in Montgomery, to begin their studies of voice and piano. Upon graduation, the bright lights and the big city beckoned, so the Conservatory of Music's enrollment was increased by the quantity of two as these two Laura Lovelies ventured out of Dixie and into the cosmopolitan river town metropolis of Cincinnati. Abner and Birdie would determine many years later this was money well spent because Evelyn sang and taught piano and voice to many students for years; and Lucy has continued with her music for well over half a century.

Rumor has it and this will *NEVER* be corroborated by the Dean girls that one of the eligible bachelors, down in South Alabama, was and aspiring young writer, named Truman Capote. Granny shared a story with me that Truman was paying a call on Lucy. Her refusal to accept his invitation for a date was based on the fact that Truman made a crucial error in that he appeared at the Dean residence one afternoon with liquor on his breath. Yes, brethren, this vile person had the audacity to partake in the drink of the devil, but the most contemptuous action was his appearance at 309 East Ida Avenue, under the influence. Needless to day, this was Truman's first and last attempt to court a Dean, and his reputation was forever cast as that of a real dandy, in lower 'Bama. Should this episode be brought to the attention of my mother she will emphatically deny any knowledge or participation in this verbally documented event that occurred during her adolescent years.

While Evelyn and Lucy attended Huntington College, they befriended Harriet Waites, from Andalusia, who was about to wed a young man from Bryn Mawr, Pennsylvania, by the name of Bill Rue. Evelyn was in the bride's court and this is when she met Bill's brother, John R. Rue IV, who was the best man. Talk about people from opposite ends of the earth. There couldn't be a broader range of socio-economic disparity than that of rural Opp, versus cosmopolitan Bryn Mawr, where the only poor folks were those who served as domestics to those families like the Rues. Well, the marriage of Evelyn and Johnny was the beginning of a relationship that would last well over fifty years - consummated in Pennsylvania, and nurtured down in Alabama.

After Evelyn and Johnny were married, they resided adjacent to the family estate, in Bryn Mawr, to be joined by other brothers and their families who lived in contiguous houses. Johnny, their brother Howdy, and Bill Rue began their married lives and the conception of many cousins commenced on that estate during the early 1940's. The Rue clan was comprised of Nona Michener Rue and John R. "Pierpop" Rue, who emanated from old Philadelphia aristocracy. Their business was shoe manufacturing and extreme wealth was derived from this family enterprise. The Rue house, which I shall never forget, was a sprawling stone mansion set on several acres of rolling Pennsylvania countryside. The kitchen, alone, was the size of some apartments while the remainder of the house is a blur in my memory.

Aunt Evelyn and Uncle Johnny remained in Bryn Mawr, for about five years while their children grew, and they eventually relocated to Opp, around 1948. Because of Uncle Johnny's association with shoe manufacturing, he decided to open a retail shoe store adjacent to Dean's Pharmacy, in Opp.

Lucille Dean in Pensacola, FL, circa 1938

CDR Henry L. Miller, circa 1940

Simultaneous, with this courtship and marriage between Evelyn Dean and John Rue, was the relationship between Lucille

Dean and one Henry L. Miller, a Navy Lieutenant, in Pensacola, Florida. After Lucy graduated from the Cincinnati Conservatory of Music she moved down to Pensacola, to begin her illustrious career as a piano teacher. Many damsels flocked to this small city to take advantage of the proliferation of eligible men of sound breeding and education. Yes, the birthplace of Naval Aviation was the home for all Naval officers who were to earn their Wings of Gold, and this was terribly exciting to those gals who were eager to expand their not-so-worldly charms and horizons. In what other town could a relatively naive damsel meet a graduate of Annapolis, a commissioned officer, an aspiring aviator, and enter that social strata of gala festivities held at Fort Barrancas Officers Club, afternoon teas at the Admirals home, squadron family outings on the whitest beaches in the world, travel to every corner of the globe, and have a relatively secure *albeit not opulent* economic foundation for the rest of their lives? So, Lucy made a wise decision and established her piano studio smack dab right in the heart of Pensacola.

Whether the marriage was consummated in the piano studio, in the Bachelor Officers' Quarters, or in the honeymoon suite, I was born, in Pensacola, on December 26, 1941. Don't remember the occasion and, as a matter of fact, didn't return to Pensacola, for twenty-two years until I entered Navy School, of Pre-Flight, Class of 29-64. Must be something in the genes that makes people yearn for the attainment of those abilities that break the surly bonds of earth, otherwise known as flight.

<u>Lucy on her honeymoon, 1939</u>

And, so began the lives of Rego and me and the germination of those families of Deans, Rues and Millers that would become the basis for these yarns and factual episodes; and to far corners of the globe - the Philippines, Pennsylvania, Hawaii, California, Mississippi, Yellowstone, Maryland, Bryn Mawr, Bethesda, Opp, Amory, Starkville, Norfolk, Yosemite, Panama City, Manila, Los Altos, Coronado, Auburn, San Francisco, and others.

I have this color-tinted photograph of my aunt and mother supposedly taken when they were about thirteen years old. The image is one of my prized possessions and it is the only one of its kind, in existence. In this image I see my genetic likeness and those of my cousins. More important, I see the eyes that portray innocence and purity, and I feel sad because I, too, was that age and of that serenity many years ago which, in some respects, seems like yesterday. My daughter, Kimberly, is thirty and she is so very different from my mother and aunt because of her urban culture and California ersatz sophistication, but she has that same twinkle in her eye, and is of that same maverick spirit. My regret is that she was unable to experience some of those marvelous aspects of my childhood spent, in Opp, during those years of innocence in the late '40's and '50's. Perhaps she will have the opportunity to visit Opp, some day when she feels it is important to her psychological development. Or, she may simply choose not to identify with the blacktop rural byways of my southern past, and to simply move on down that smooth California concrete urban interstate with her present life.

One of these days I'll travel to Georgiana, and research the Barganier family tree. The only recollection of ancestry from the maternal side of my family is that we are descendents of William Henry Harrison, ninth President of the United States. Other than that legacy I am not familiar with the remaining family descendants, alive or deceased, who comprise the genetics on the maternal Dean side of our family tree.

My Aunt Evelyn passed away in the early '80s and, with her, another member of a generation that will be forever lost within the next twenty years. Loosing my aunt was a severe blow not only to me but, also, to my mother because Aunt Evelyn was the only remaining link to her childhood. The two of them were real pals throughout life and they relied on each other for support whenever the going got rough. Evelyn remained in the South until her death, raising her three children who have, also, decided to remain in Dixie through their careers and marriages; Rego, in Marietta, GA and Stevie and Carol, in Richmond, VA.

John Rue, circa 1975

Evelyn's husband, Uncle Johnny, is, also, deceased. His last years were spent holed up in a nursing home, in Amory, but I recollect only vivid and cheerful images of my favorite uncle - not his demise in those awful convalescent homes where we place our relatives so they can die, in obscurity. We last visited in 1974, while he was in retirement, and enjoying good health. Johnny reminded me so much of Arnold Palmer, the famous golfer, in his mannerisms and his physical appearance. And coincidentally, both he and Palmer hail from Pennsylvania. But, mostly, I remember Uncle Johnny selling shoes to everyone in Covington county.

My stepson recently started part time work at a women's shoe store, in San Francisco, and he had some interesting comments after his first day on the job. His quote, "The women are beautiful and the gals couldn't wait for my assisting them while trying on new pairs of the latest shoe fashions. Wonder if it had anything to do with my soft hands, and roving eyes?" A shoe salesman's job is not unlike that of a woman's physician in that one can, perhaps, gain a different view of the world from the vantage point of being physically situated below the sitting position of the female customers. In other words, opportunities to look up a woman's dress not only become numerous but, in addition, almost a given part of the operation.

To our surprise, Uncle Johnny, our family shoe salesman, knew almost every woman in Opp, and I suspect that he could have divulged many secrets and medical theories pertaining to these damsels' lifestyles had he been the type who would spill Macy's secret plans to Gimbels. He, too, must have possessed the soft touch and the ability to view forbidden sights while maintaining lowered eyelids and neutral facial expressions.

Uncle Johnny was just one of the guys. He simply had to be especially with two sons, like Rego and Stevie. One night Rego, just starting as a high school freshman, was sitting in the kitchen while having some supper with Evelyn and Johnny. Uncle Johnny suddenly asked Rego if he could borrow a couple of dollars because he was short of cash. Rego obliged by indicating that he may have a few dollars, so he proceeded to stand up from the table and remove his wallet from the back pocket of his Levis. As Rego opened the billfold to search for the folded money a condom fell out of the folds, and landed on top of his shoe. Rego's eyes never left those of his fathers, but he knew what had just occurred. As Rego tried to keep from breaking out into a cold sweat, his eyes still glued on those of his dad's, he quickly thought of how to camouflage this embarrassing predicament. Rego quickly handed his father as dollar, or two, and then he proceeded to stiff-leg his way from the kitchen into another neutral room without lifting his foot where the condom was resting off the floor while locking his eyes with those of his dad. This was the only way that Rego could escape this situation and not have the condom fall from the top of his shoe to the floor directly in front of Uncle Johnny.

Back at 309 East Ida Avenue

"That's it, you two, let's get the film up to Virginia's for processing so we can get another poster blown up when I get back to San Francisco. I'll get us each a large black and white to frame because I seriously doubt if we'll get back here to do this again any time real soon, do you think?"

Don't suppose I want to see this place again, ever. The house is gone, my grandparents are gone, the neighbors are gone. Everyone's dead. Everything but the memories are gone. Memories of sneaking out to go down to the Sweet Shoppe. Memories of accidentally swallowing a chunk of chewing tobacco while we worked on the milk truck that one summer. The daily movie matinees and the municipal pool. All the good things we did before we were old enough to get into real trouble at the Park More Drive In with liquor and sleazy broads. Sweet, sweet memories of the families and Granny and Daddy Dean's friends whose names are now a blur.

I remember the hush, the peaceful quiet of Opp now that I stop to think about it. No blaring boom boxes and loud neighbors and obnoxious generation x types with their cellular phones, beepers, and chirpy auto alarms disturbing the natural sounds of the cats and dogs and goats and the hoofs of the horse-drawn buckboards coming down Ida Avenue occasionally. I loved the sounds of the lightening and thunderstorms during the summer. I loved the sound of Miriam Donaldson practicing her trumpet early in the afternoons.

I loved the unabated silence…

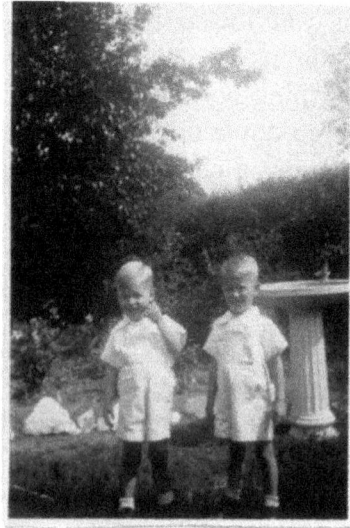

Rego and Panky in Granny's backyard, circa 1945

Vacation Bible School Dropouts!

"You two, Rego and Panky, have been hangin'. 'round this house for days now, and I'm beginnin' to believe that y'all is bored. Everytime I gets to sit down to shell these field peas you two are naggin' me with a thousand questions 'bout what's for dinner, or anything special for dessert, or how do I tie this bandana 'round my hair. Lordy Almighty, I can find dozens of chores for you to do like sweepin' the sidewalk and the front porch. Swimmin' pool ain't open for the season yet, and you're too young to go get jobs, so I'm recommendin' to yo mothers that you go to Vacation Bible School, up at the First Baptist. 'Sides, it'll do you good to have somethin' to occupy your time with somethin' all boys need more of, and that's old time religion."

This individual doing all the preaching was Ro Ceil who was

addressing us in a very stern voice. Ro Ceil was Granny's maid, our nanny. She had been with Granny for quite a while and we have lots of respect for her. I came down from Norfolk, where my dad is stationed in the Navy. My school year ended a week before Rego's so I'm here with my grandparents waiting for the municipal pool to open and looking forward to the afternoon matinees at the Royal Theater and the Dixie Drive In.

"Aw, Ro Ceil, we'd rather play at the clay quarry or go fishing with Daddy Dean, or anything but Vacation Bible School! Please don't say anything about this to our mothers. We promise to stay out of trouble and to clean our plates at dinner if you'll let this notion slip away. Please? Please? Pretty please?"

As we beg for mercy, we realize that our pleas were truly in vain. Sometime later that day my mother approached Rego and me about this very same subject. "Rego, Panky. Evelyn and I agree that you two should attend Vacation Bible School this summer, and don't put up any argument. You're going whether you like it or not. Panky, since you're Catholic, you can say your Catholic prayers and not say the Baptist prayers, if you feel that way. Nonetheless, the school starts at nine o'clock in the morning and goes until noon. We'll get you up in plenty of time to clean up and to have some breakfast."

Mom's word appears to be gospel and our whimpering, sobbing and general complaining was useless. Aunt Evelyn's and Mom's minds are made up and that's that. Next morning we dragged ourselves out of bed, moped around with gloomy faces and report to the first floor of the First Baptist Church for our first class which is a first-class pain in the ass. Our teacher is the typical southern evangelical, even-tempered, middle-aged man whose mission is to train youngun's in the rudiments of Christianity. He is also the store manager at Moore's Economy Store, just around the corner.

This is where we learn to hum the timeless classic, "Yes, Jesus loves me. Yes, Jesus, loves me. Yes, Jesus loves me. The

Bible tells me so."

Our little contemporaries appeared to love this school. Rego and I had our minds made up that we weren't going to like it, period. We tried to do the small projects assigned and to have fun, but no such luck. Our minds were at the swimming pool and at the matinees but they were not at the First Baptist Church Vacation Bible School. Eventually, I came up and whisper to Rego that we could escape through the window in the teacher's office. He can't believe his little ears because this is desertion, a crime worse than death. Never in our young lives had we done such a dastardly deed, but there was always a first. The teacher warned us on several occasions to behave, or face the consequences. Of course, our pip-squeak little classmates thought this was hysterical and giggled incessantly. I asked Rego when we were going to bolt for the window and make our heroic escape. He said that we will quietly leave the big room where we were doing the two "P's" - playing and praying - and go into our teacher's office, close the door, open the window, step out between the bushes, and run down the street. Since the class was on the first floor there wasn't going to be a problem of scaling down a wall or anything dangerous. My major problem was with the time. How were we going to explain being home early or being caught uptown at Daddy Dean's pharmacy when our folks know that we are supposed to still be in school?

The time had finally come to make our move. Rego grabbed my arm and we both walked into our teacher's private office. We slowly close the door and eaked towards the open window across the room. Our pulses raced and we were on the verge of peeing in our britches. Suddenly, Rego made his move and stepped over the sill and lowered himself onto the grass outside. I quickly grabbed the sash and yanked the top window down, and locked it so Rego coukldn't get back inside.

The last thing I heard uttered from Rego's lips was, "Panky, you little prick. I'm going to kill you when you get home. You raise this window right now, y'hear."

I reentered the main room where all the kids are working on their projects. Suddenly, one of my classmates opened the door of the private office and saw Rego running down the street. She ran back into our room and yelled at the top of her voice, "Rego's jumped out the window and is running down the streeeeeeet!" A flurry of the kids scurried for the door just in time to see Rego rounding the corner of the church. I started giggling and then laughed to the point where I was choking.

Our teacher's parting words to me were as follows, "Panky you tell Rego that my phone call to his folks will beat him home by about fifteen minutes, just enough time for his daddy to get out his leather belt and teach him a lesson that Rego and Jesus will never forget. And, by the way, tell him not to bother to return to Bible School tomorrow. We'll get along just fine without him."

Rego, for all of his eight years, was already heading down the road of truancy. He had no idea of the consequences until the door opened at his house with Uncle Johnny waiting with a disgusted look on his face and his leather strap in his hands.

For once, I made the correct decision in staying at school. Lordy knows how that belt must have felt on Rego's butt. Rumor had it that he was given the ultimatum to toe the line or else, for the remainder of that summer. In the meantime I had to find a way to keep Rego from beating the shit out of me for locking that window behind him.

A highway billboard with the large letters indicates the summer has again arrived and it's time to get those chillun into learning about the Lord. "Please call for registration information."

I think of Rego, and how terribly disappointed Roy and Dale must have been.

First Baptist Church Vacation Bible School Begins June 1st.

Rego, don't be late!

<u>Sneaking Out</u>

Granny's playhouse was located in her backyard at the house on Ida Avenue. Granny and Daddy Dean had this separate structure built away from the main house when Aunt Evelyn and my mother, Lucy, were still small girls in Opp, so they would have a place to play with their dolls. The playhouse consists of one small room with painted walls, a wooden floor, an overhead light, and a gas burning fake log fireplace. I'd say it was about three times as long as the bed and the ceiling was rather high, a lot higher than I was used to. The remnants from several large fig trees adorn the roof whenever that time of the season arrived and the branches dropped rotten fruit onto the shiny tin metal and gutters. There was a rather large bamboo grove with shoots growing clear up to the sky next to the playhouse so you couldn't see the chicken coup next door at the Donaldson's. The path from the back door leading from the kitchen to the playhouse was dirt, when dry, or red clay mud when wet. There was only one window in the entire building, and a crabapple bush covered the view, just outside.

Rego and I loved the playhouse because it was our playhouse now that our mothers had grown up and moved away from the main house. Granny often used it for her floral business but she would rearrange it as our guest room whenever I came down visiting during the summers. A big brass bed sat squarely in the middle of the room, leaving precious little space for anything else, such as a dresser or a vanity.

Day in and day out, Rego and I rushed to the playhouse to change into our bathing suits for the race down to the municipal pool. Or, we perform the daily ritual of afternoon naps required by our parents, just after the noon dinner. Then, we finally crashed onto the brass bed every night, but not before we stood in the doorway to pee onto the surrounding bushes rather than go all the way into the house, and to the bathroom, like civilized young boys, don't you know.

Earlier in the day we each consumed about five bags of Fireball's boiled peanuts. Suppose we should have eaten only a bag but we couldn't stop. Digestion had commenced and the flagitious event was enough to send a mushroom-shaped cloud into the stratosphere had someone dare light a match anywhere near our room. Airburst after airburst, and none more evocative or pungent than its predecessor, as the pastoral silence of the evening was interrupted by the anal cornucopia of orchestral melodies not unlike those emitted by large animals fed on unrestricted daily diets of alfalfa or barley. Rego and I released enough gaseous fumes to provide natural energy for all of the Alabama Rural Power Commission.

After the farting subsided and we are able to gather our thoughts we made a pledge that the following night we'd pretend like we were fast asleep when Granny came out to check up on us. Then, in the dead of night, we would ever so quietly slip into our jeans and sneak around the corner to the back alley and make our way by the light of that same silvery moon up town to get ourselves a hamburger at the Sweet Shoppe.

Morning was here and we asked Granny for a jar of Vaseline in order to soothe the anal chaffing that resulted from our biological ingestion, digestion, and flagitious release of those goddamned boiled peanuts that we loved so much, and the ones we simply couldn't stop eating. It was going to be a race to the toilet I could predict all day long except for when we go to the pool.

We were exhausted and Granny told us to hit the sack. I waited until the coast was clear and I shook Rego's shoulder so that he woke up. It was time to get up, get dressed, and make our way silently back to the alley. We slipped into our jeans and t-shirts and ever so slowly opened the screen door so that Granny wouldn't hear the squeaking of the rusty springs thus coming out to check up on us. Our eyes were becoming adjusted to the moonlight and we ran back by the bamboo patch and into the alley only to be greeted by the furry creatures around the neighbor's garbage cans which had been strewn up and down the one-lane dirt path as the little critters screeched and meowed in the light of the full moon. In about another hundred feet we reached the paved street, and our first real challenge to determine if we could elude the lights of the few cars to continue our trek uptown. We stood in the bushes while a lone car drove by and then we bolted across the street to another alley, and more stench and screeching cats.

By now we had this escape and evasion routine down pat, so we let our guards down and proceeded up Ida Avenue along the sidewalk as we hid behind the huge oak trees when the lights of the few oncoming cars approached us. In another two blocks we'd reach Main Street and our ultimate destination, the Sweet Shoppe.

We rounded the corner of Dean's Pharmacy and slithered along the store fronts so that the local police would not see us lurking in the shadows as we inched our way for about another hundred feet, or about four more storefronts. Whew! That was a close one past the pool hall! And, the Opp cop was heading our way in his black and white patrol car but he failed to capture us in his peripheral vision. At last, we opened the screen door to the entrance of the cafe and we were greeted by Miriam, the one and only waitress at this hour of the morning, who blurted out, "Rego. Panky. What in the dickens are y'all doing here at this time of the morning? Your mamas and Granny Dean will whip your butts if they catch you down here! Lawdy, I bet you two snuck out of your grandmother's and thought that a burger and shake in the middle of the night was just what you needed. Am I right, you two?"

Our eyes were as big as silver dollars, and we were silent, and the looks on our faces caused her and the few diners to burst out laughing. We stared in hopes that we would not be turned over to our folks. All we wanted was some food. All we wanted was cheeseburgers, French fries and chocolate malts. Silently we ate before paying the tab and retracing our steps back down Main Street and the dark alleys towards the playhouse. We were scared to death that the Opp cop would drop in, apprehend us, and take us back to Granny's in the back seat of the squad car. Just when we thought the coast was clear two patrolmen walked over to the counter, sat down, and ordered coffee. I began to tremble and Rego started to slide under the table. I grabbed him and hold him next to me so the police could see both of us if they wanted. They began to talk with Miriam and she kept their attention as we emptied our pockets of change to pay the bill. Slowly, we made our way to the door so the police wouldn't turn around to see us. We made it safely outside and scurried around to the alley and hid up against the brick wall before deciding to head on back to Granny's.

The full moon that helped guide us had gone behind a cloud, so our return was slower and more intense than coming uptown an hour earlier. My eyes were as wide open as they can possibly get and I kept an ear tuned in for sounds of night creatures lurking in the alleyways and behind the huge oak trees lining the streets. Hardly a car was on the road and it was dead silent along our path towards home.

Another musical trip as we broke wind on this, otherwise, breeze-free evening as quiet as they come with the exception of our repetitive farts and burps that echoed off the corrugated surfaces of the garbage cans, tin sheds, and into the open bedroom windows of our neighbors. But, these folks were none the wiser as they were awakened by the ear-shattering dawn alert signaled by numerous roosters signalling another hot summer morning in Opp.

Mom, Granny Dean and Me Mclean Gardens, DC circa 1946

Traveling with Lucy

The eastern seaboard conjures up many thoughts when it comes to lifestyles, food, weather, the seasons, mentality, diction, and clothing. I associate this region with a class system or, as they have in Hindu societies, a caste system, that delineates the haves from the have-nots. Oddly enough, this measurement isn't made just in terms of monetary wealth possessed by the famous families of this region but, also, in genealogy. Who were your grandparents? Where were they from? Where did your parents attend school? Do you have a summer place on the Cape or on the Chesapeake? Andover, Class of '39, mind you.

I have always found the region from Boston, down to North Carolina, to be special and to be as integral part of my youth while growing up in Washington, and in the suburb of nearby Bethesda. As I indicated previously, Mom's only sister, Aunt Evelyn, married a man from the North, specifically Pennsylvania. Uncle Johnny's lineage went as far back as the original Michener family, including James, the famous author. Johnny, his two brothers, and their respective spouses, all resided near the family property in Bryn Mawr, a suburb of Philadelphia.

Little did I know that the Rue family estate was literally huge, visually pleasing, and grandiose. The interior consisted of a kitchen the size of today's Levittown houses, and the rest of the house seemed to go on forever. The surrounding property consisted of acres of rolling hills, barns, and picket fences - similar to a Norman Rockwell image on canvass. The three Rue sons- Johnny, Billy and Howdy- live on a cul-de-sac on what was formerly the Buck estate. Talk about being set up with an upper crust lifestyle by one's parents. These three lads had it made in the shade. Living on the pastoral estate, rent free, in the splendor of Bryn Mawr.

My cousin, Rego, shy of my age by of nine months, Aunt Evelyn, uprooted from her native southern Alabama, and her husband, Uncle Johnny, settled in adjacent to the Rue estate and were in the process of making babies. I simply couldn't wait for the day when Rego, who was Johnny and Evelyn's first offspring, and I could visit one another, and run around those wide open fields and experience an almost surreal vacation - days larger than life itself and chock full of one adventure after the next.

My parents and I lived in McLean Gardens Apartments in Washington, D.C., in the area known as Spring Valley. This was a huge apartment complex consisting of dozens of two-story, red brick colonial-style buildings and each building housed ten apartments. These buildings looked exactly the same and we chillun constantly knocked on the wrong door, in the wrong building, in the wrong complex, forever lost. My life consisted of nursery school, then kindergarten, then first grade at the elite Miss Libby's Elementary School, over on fashionable Connecticut Avenue. Living in a complex like McLean Gardens may sound like oodles of fun for a pip-squeak, but it wasn't. Most of the denizens were transitory so we hardly had the opportunity to socialize before the pending migrations to other towns or housing complexes in the area. In other words, there weren't any kids to play with! A shitty situation, to say the least. My thoughts turned to playing hide and seek and trying to catch butterflies during the day, and fireflies during the evening.

The choo-choo train that clickety-clacked from Washington's Central Station to Philadelphia's Main Terminal was something very special in my life. Whenever my folks and I traveled up to Bryn Mawr, we took this train, usually the one scheduled to depart in the early evening, just in time for supper on board. Those were the days when the various travelers checked on board, found their seats or compartments, and asked the porter to make their reservations for a particular seating in the dining car. The porter, a black man, dressed in a meticulously starched jacket, lint-free and perfectly creased black trousers, and spit-shined shoes, would ask if we had a special time in mind for supper.

Central Station, in Washington, was god-awful big and overwhelming in scale. To any six year old, the building appeared to be the largest thing on earth. The hallways were as wide as streets, the main lobby as big as a football field and as high as the inside of a dirigible hangar. Voices echoed in the great hall and the resonance of thousands of travelers added to the drama as we located our track where the shiny stainless steel clad cars were located. Steam poured from under the various cars and engines statically parked on adjacent tracks; and the ominous patina of the tracks, the soot from the locomotives and the inadequate lighting provided quite a spectacular contrast to the gleaming sides of the Pullmans and the locomotives. Climbing up the chromed steel stepladder into the assigned car was a step into fantasy as we left reality back in McLean Gardens.

"All Abooaarrd," shouted the porter, and the steam began to pour from under the steel wheels as we slowly inched away from the station. I was so excited that we were finally leaving and heading north, towards Philadelphia, and towards my cousins who seemed light years away. But, my appetite wasn't light years away! Mom and I couldn't wait to repair to the dining car for supper because we knew the food served on board was special, and we longed for the excitement of the occasion. Most of the food prepared in those days was from scratch cooking with very little prior preparation, or use of frozen foods. The soups were especially delicious and the desserts were freshly prepared, and simply yummy. Didn't really care about the entrees, which usually consisted of a chicken dish or a roast beef plate. But, I distinctly remember those soups and desserts were well worth the trip.

"Mizz Miller, time for yo' seatin' in the dinin' car. Can I assist you with yo' son while we walk through the cars towards the dinin' car? This train is mighty rough just as we is passin' through rough parts of these tracks," said the porter.

"Please, porter, I always seem to have trouble navigating through these slamming doors between the cars. And, I seem to lose my footing on the slippery metal floors. Panky, you hold my hand tight and we'll get going towards that proverbial last car which is always that dining car. Why can't they put the dining car next to ours so we won't have to go through so many of these confounded doors?"

Why! Why! Why! Why was it that my mother always had to complain about situations that I considered to be challenging and adventurous? Hell, I thought this was fun with a capital "F." This old train moved like a hula dancer-left to right with sudden jerks, right to left with the same momentum-coupled with the screeching brakes and the steam pouring under the wheels. Passengers on the move, going all sorts of places to visit with all sorts of people, peering out the windows at the city as we made our way into the countryside heading towards Baltimore. At last, the dining car was within sight and olfactory recognition.

Have you ever experienced the mixture of food cooking and metal scraping against metal, coupled with steam emissions? It is a peculiar combination, similar to that of being aboard a ship at sea. To some travelers, it is rather nauseating while others consider this aroma to be stimulating and a sign of adventure, of travel, of something foreign to the senses. Anyway, I absolutely loved it and I still enjoy the sensation whenever I'm aboard a vessel with this concoction of odors and aromas that I consider to be a sensual aphrodisiac for this eternal adolescent.

"I'm Messus Milla, and we have reservations for 6:15. Is our table ready?" asked Mom.

The maitre'd replied, "You'll have to wait for about five minutes while the waiter clears the table, ma'am."

"Please hurry so we can sit down. This rocking and rolling has my nerves in a tizzy. Furthermore, we're hungry so we'd appreciate anything you can do."

"This way, folks, and you, young man, can sit here next to the window so you can look out at the pretty sights."

Traveling with my mother, when I was young, was probably one of the primary reasons why I am so accustomed as an adult to delays, inconveniences, and other misfortunes associated with travel logistics. She was not what I consider a mentor in this regard but, rather, an example of what not to do in order to cir-cumvent adverse conditions. Mom had this way about her that most folks found brusque and a wee bit abrasive. Perhaps, she learned this behavior from her mother, Granny Dean, who had little if any patience with those in the travel industry.

Having said that, we enjoyed our suppers and I simply didn't want to leave that dining car because this is where I might see some other boys my age. Problem with this situation is that it usually turned out to be a very short-term friendship . . . only a few hours before we'd reach our destinations and step off the train. So, most of the times, I would go back to our car and stare out the window at the telephone poles zipping by the farms and tractors and hay stacks as the evening mist rose off the fields to

54

form a low-flying gray haze during the sunsets.

"Next stop, Philadelphia Central Station in about fifteen minutes, ladies and gentlemen. Please gather your belongings and prepare to disembark promptly upon arrival," the porter bellowed as he walked up and down the narrow isles the length of each car, both Pullman and coach. This is the time when Mom would begin to get fidgety and start to verbalize about the problems that she would create in her mind. "What if Evelyn and Johnny have the times of our arrival mixed up? What if no one is there to meet us at the station? How long of a drive is it to the house in Bryn Mawr? Wonder how much traffic there is this time of the night?" She would slowly begin to drive me crazy with her worrywart behavior. And, she worried about nothing. Never had a problem. Everyone was always on time. The ride out to the country was effortless. For sure, I can tell you that my trait of being worried about inconsequential details stems from a formidable instructor, called Mom.

"Aunt Evelyn, Uncle Johnny, where's Rego? Didn't he come with you to the station? I want to see him so bad. How long will the ride be until we get home?" *Here I was trying to impersonate my mother with these rapid-fire questions.*

"Panky, Lucille, so good to see y'all. Let's get your bags and get on down the road. Did you have any problems on the trip or was it as smooth as I remember it last time we came down to see y'all in Washington?" was Johnny's greeting to us.

"Evelyn, that train was the roughest thing you've ever seen. We could barely walk down the isles to go to the bathroom and to the dining car. Well, I almost turned around, went back to my seat and skipped supper rather than slip and slide all over those metal floors connecting the cars."

"Shucks, Aunt Evelyn, I had a good time on the train. Should have seen what we had for supper. Boy, the soup was good, too, but I loved the pecan pie with the big pile of vanilla ice cream on top. Sure wish you could have been with us. Maybe next time we can take a trip together and I know that you will enjoy the train as much as I did."

"Panky, we'd love to do that sometime but, right now, we need to get your bags and head on up the road. Rego was pestering me to death about getting you up here," said Evelyn.

We left downtown Philadelphia, and were soon back in the country heading for Bryn Mawr. The green rolling hills with the mansion and horse barns with white fences stuck out in my mind. Lots of open space and trees and birds and everything appeared larger than life to me. You see, I lived in an apartment complex. Row after row of these three story, red brick, buildings that looked the same. Fact remains where Bryn Mawr was the antithesis of McLean Gardens, which is one reason for my vivid recollections of the magnificent beauty of the Rue property.

Now, we're talking very, very big when we refer to the Rue house. It was definitely what you would call a mansion. Stone construction, sitting on at least an acre of front yard alone, not counting the property behind and down the road. And the kitchen was immense with the huge stone fireplace, central island the size of today's condominiums, and other living areas that dwarfed not only this pip-squeak but, also, floor plans and room dimensions that we consider spacious by today's standards. Of course, when you're only four feet tall everything seemed large, overpowering, sometimes scary, and often mysterious simply because we viewed the world as if we were looking at everyone's kneecaps. Get above the knees and the waist and, wow, is this person big, or what!

When Walt Disney designed his first amusement park, Disneyland, he perceived this to be a problem for the little tykes. He didn't want to make the children afraid of large objects so his solution was a brilliant one. All of the structures in Disneyland were designed and constructed on four-fifths scale. Hence, when you view the buildings and other structures, such as the riverboats, they appear to be in scale for the smaller guests in the park. Brilliant strategy, design, and marketing.

The three houses, situated side-by-side, sat on a cul-de-sac on the Buck estate. Howdy, Billy, and Uncle Johnny, and their respective families, occupied these houses. All three of the Rue sons assumed the role of modern urban sharecroppers who left each morning for work while their wives remained home to raise the babies. All three of my cousins - Rego, Stevie, Carol - and I were inseparable. We ate together, bathed together, played together, got into trouble together, slept together, had pillow fights together.

"Panky, let's go down to the quarry where the old barn is standing, and play cowboys and Indians. What do you say?" Rego would ask over and over while we sat at breakfast.

"Let's go, Rego. Do I need my shoes or can we run barefoot?"

"Don't need no shoes, and I can beat you down there!"

Two bolts of toe-headed, four-foot, lightening shot out of the kitchen at full speed blazing through the moist green grass of the rolling meadows out of sight of the house. *Scenes from a Norman Rockwell painting are forever imprinted in my memory, and we were, most likely, two good candidates for his subjects depicting Americana in those early years.* Over the grass knoll sat the remains of a large building with the steel girders rising to the sky, rusting away from the elements. We would spend hours climbing over those beams only to discover, on one occasion, nests of green hornets just waiting to pounce. Those little buggers reminded us of the comic strip "The Green Hornet," so we expected some sort of magical drama to unfold with human characters wearing green capes and masks but, instead, we got the real McCoy, stingers and all!

The humming of these little monster produced a lasting impression; thousands, perhaps millions, of them swooping down on us, as this noise in my ears became almost intolerable.

"Boys, we're having lots of kids over late this afternoon for our Fourth of July picnic so you will be meeting boys and girls from around the area, and some from Philadelphia. They'll serve hot dogs, hamburgers, my famous potato salad, plus tons of Kool Aid. Later in the day we'll break out the horses and ponies and have an old fashioned hay ride over to the large barn on the back property." Rego's paternal gramdma Nona Rue was in charge of the day's activities and it was apparent that she was in full control of the situation. Rego and I started to meet the other boys and girls as the vast consumption of Forth of July stomach cramp food began. Certainly, our parents must have been worn out just watching their darling little children in a kinetic mode with absolutely no obvious signs of winding down.

In addition, we had the company of several teenagers who acted as babysitters and monitors for those of us too young to mount a pony or to reach the step up into the hay wagon. You could almost hear Lucy and Evelyn in the background saying, "Those two boys are certain to get hurt today with the way they're running around, jumping up on the top rails of the fences, and teasing the horses and ponies. Lordy, they're going to have such stomachaches tonight from eating everything in sight. I'm simply exhausted just from watching them. Maybe they'll begin to settle down after their digestive tracts take over, and the metamorphosis begins with the conversion of all that junk into nutrition that has to do some good, whatever it is!" These two women were in perpetual conflict with the universe. Our mothers failed to realize that children, of all ages, took chances-some more dangerous or challenging than others-but chances, nonetheless. So, our attitudes were to ignore their plebeian pleas for calm and order and, instead, we implemented what we were best at. And, my friends, that was chaos and confusion.

Our stomachs were full and the sun had set and the chill of the early evening air prompted us to ask the older members of the group if we could go into the barn for a story. Their reply was an overwhelming "Yes," because of the ease in monitoring our whereabouts and hopes that we would settle down and relax for once! After all, we had worn these grown-ups into total fatigue so they were extremely receptive to any suggestion involving rest and relaxation! One of our favorite teenagers asked if any of us had heard of <u>Rumplestiltskin</u> and we replied in unison, "No." What in the hell was a Rumplestiltskin anyway? Some sort of nut, or fruitcake, or monster? Well, we were about to find out.

Images of ancient Europe, of kings and queens, of surfs and farms, of mysteries that appeared larger than life were described as our young girl storyteller mesmerized us with her voice while reading this classic folk tale. All we could hear besides her voice was the occasional belching of the calves and the whinnies of the horses as we lay in the barn amidst the hay and the dim lighting, watching the moon rise up over the hills. Our eyes were as large as our imaginations as we stayed tuned into each and every word she spoke while the tale of the peasant weaving straw into gold was delivered precisely as if the storyteller had done this a hundred times previously, which she most likely had.

One by one, we felt as if there were magnets in the ground below acting as negative polarization in conflict with the positive ions resting on our little eyelids. In summary, we were tired as hell, so the tune "Babes in Toyland" started to hum its melody in our ears. *Can't begin to tell you the last time when I was at peace with the universe as much as I was this special evening. I suppose the child in every one of us yearns for an occasional nurturing and for a feeling that the universe is in harmony, by seizing that very special moment.*

"Evelyn, suppose we should go down to the barn, gather up the youngin's, and take them back to the house. Can you remember the last time when they played as hard as today? By the

59

way, Johnny, this is one of the tastiest cocktails I've had in ages. What did you do to make it so special, or is it simply because I haven't experienced one of your Perfect Rob Roys before?"

"Lucy, bless you, sweet thing, for the compliment and no, this is the first time I've made this kind of drink. A Perfect Rob Roy is similar to those I concocted but with a few modifications in the ingredients. They get even better after the second or third."

"Lordy mercy, Johnny, I'll be on my knees walking back to the house if I have another one. Anyway, like I said, we should go get the boys before the evening chill sets in and they catch a death of a cold. Funny thing. It sure isn't chilly out now. Must have been close to ninety today, so we shouldn't worry too much about it getting down near freezing. Let me finish this marvelous cocktail and we'll be off."

"Panky, sure have had fun with you and I want you to come back up and see me real soon, okay? And, when you do, be sure to bring a cape and a mask so we can dress up and go back down to that old barn and play 'The Green Hornet.' Mommy was saying something about us moving down to Opp, soon."

"Mommy, where'll we live if we move down to Opp.? I mean, will we stay close to Panky?"

"Panky, we'll be staying in Silver Springs, just about half hour away from your apartment, in McLean Gardens. Uncle Johnny and the rest of us have decided to move down to Opp, because Johnny wants to open his own business down there. So, we'll get ourselves situated for a while in Silver Springs, then mosey down to Opp. I think I'm just as excited as you are because we'll be close to your mom and dad. I miss Hank and Lucy so much when I don't get to see them often. This way, we can see y'all, and you and Rego can still get into all sorts of mischief."

Unfortunately, it was time to start traveling again with Lucy.

Just the thought of getting on that train and listening to my very own mother whine and complain and bitch about the noise of the train, the smell of the train, the motion of the train, the porters of the train, and the dining car's location on the train was about all this kid could take. So, like I did so many times previously, I shut out any outside interference by merely tuning out what I didn't want to hear. No, didn't have any trouble hearing. As a matter of fact I could perceive decibel ratings of a tiny little ant sleeping, but only if I wanted to. To this day, I have an uncanny ability to detect faint sounds imperceptible to most folks around me. And, at the same time, can't hear a damn thing if I don't want to. Suppose I tuned out my parents on more than one occasion. But, the humming of the wheels on the tracks was a sound that I simply didn't want to.

Funny how long that ride from the station out to Bryn Mawr appeared when Mom and I arrived just a few days ago. Now, that we had to leave my favorite family the ride seemed to take only a few minutes for us to travel the distance back into downtown Philadelphia, for that trip back to Washington. My mood always turned sour and I definitely experienced what is referred to as an attitude check, which, roughly translated, meant I was in a piss poor frame of mind. . As a child I quickly learned to suppress my emotions and not dilly-dally around with good-byes. A simple hug from my cousins, a kiss from my aunt and uncle, and a poker-faced, glaring-at-the-ground expression was my way of indicating my disapproval of the separation from those I loved.

"All Abooaarrd," cried the Southern Crescent penguin - the black man in the white coat. "Watch yo' step, madam and you, young man, help yo' mother with her bags. Time's a wastin'. We pull out of the station in about two minutes, so you can show yo' mother to her seat in car number two, seats 35A and B."

"Panky, our car is about three cars down, as usual. Every time I ask for seats near the dining car they put us up near the locomotive. I'm going to write someone when we return and express my dissatisfaction with this entire train service. Can't they ever get anything right?"

The Primary reason why I am so misaligned today is because of those friggin' knickers!

Bull of the Woods

Sounds of early morning, like Billy goats turning over the trash cans back in the alleys searching for last night's dinner, and Cheerios. Dogs barking way off in the distance making it nearly impossible to tell whose dog it is, so that later on in the morning you could get even by shooting that "dawg" in the butt with your Daisy BB gun. The milk truck making its rounds as it pulls up to each house, puts on the brake, and exchanges full bottles of the white stuff for empties left out the night before.

Lordy, is it that time already, or can I sleep in for just a few more minutes? Granny'll surely be up and at 'em so that she can get started on making the casket sprays and other floral arrangements for the orders that she needs to fill. Still cool in the house but it'll turn into a scorcher later when the sun gets a chance to radiate through that metal roof, down through the walls, and finally into my room. Sure does feel cool and comfortable now though. Think I'll just lay here and conjure up what Rego and I'll do today after he comes over to play.

Gladdy Mae, Granny's maid, hadn't arrived at the house and that meant breakfast was a ways off. In time, she would surely get me up to issue the ultimatum that breakfast would be served in ten minutes, and to freshen up *NOW*. I'd jump out of bed, run

63

into the bathroom to pee, and to find my shorts or Levis, so that I could go visit with Granny for a few minutes to help her with her flowers.

I can hear rumblings in the back alley, probably some of the goats that broke loose during the night. I absolutely love goats. Goats of all colors, breeds, and coats. All sizes and shapes, with and without their little horns. Rego and I had our very own goat a couple of years earlier. One day, Granny drove us out into the country to deliver some flowers for a country funeral, and the farmer repaid her with a Billy goat. We put that goat in the back of Granny's car and headed back to town. As soon as we arrived, Gladdy Mae took us in tow and told us to take that goat into the back yard, tie it up, and get a bowl of Cheerios for food. That old goat loved Cheerios, your shoes, field peas still in the shell, and anything else it could get its little mouth around. Damn thing woke us up every morning before dawn as it deliberately crashed into cars, the sides of houses, and attempted to break down the back door into Granny's kitchen. Suppose he just wanted attention and lots of food. That Billy goat lasted about one week at the house, then back to the country, once and for all.

"Panky, you old sweet thang, how would you and Rego like to work with Mr. Presley on the milk truck every morning? He'll pay you each a dollar a day and he told me that he needs some help with the cases of milk that are getting too heavy for him to shuttle back and forth between his truck and the houses. Besides, you two could stand a little diversion from that swimming pool every day. Do you both some good to work with Mr. Presley so that you'll have some extra spending money this summer. I'll ask him exactly what time he'll arrive so you two boys will be ready."

Rego and I look at each other and say, "What do you think? Suppose it's a good idea and I'm kinda excited about working on that truck. I've never really been on too many trucks. You know, it doesn't have any doors so you hold onto a handle and stand in the doorway while he drives. Shoot, I think we'll have a hooting good time tomorrow, except for the fact we have to get up in the dark to get dressed. Means Granny'll probably have us go to bed early so we can get a good night's sleep, don't you think?"

Today would be a special day. Today would be a day of infamy for me. Today would progress into one of the worst days of my pathetic little life.

"Panky, here comes Butch now. Butch was our best friend and he lived just down the street from Grannys.

"Hey, Bracke, what do you think about Panky and me working for old man Presley on the milk truck tomorrow? He pays us a dollar each a day and it's 'bout a two week job before school starts.

"Do you each realize what time you have to get up? That's the bad news. The good news is that one of the last stops is at Zeb's Bakery, uptown, and you'll get some of their hot glazed donuts, right out of the oven, piping hot. Couple of those donuts with some cold milk and maybe I'll get up after all to meet you up there because my mouth's watering just thinking about it.

Every morning about this time Daddy Dean finished his morning constitutional and came out on the front porch to wait for his ride uptown to play dominos. "Hey, Daddy Dean, what do you think about Rego and me working on the milk truck, starting tomorrow morning? Saw you sitting out here on the glider and you look like you want some company, so here we are, your three favorite kids. By the way, can we have some change for Cokes at the drugstore?"

"Sure, boys." He reaches into his pocket and digs out a few pennies. "You'll like Mr. Presley, and working for him on the truck. Work never hurt anyone, and I started long before you on the farm, which meant we worked everyday, from sun up through sundown. While you're up at the drugstore having a Coke pick me up a box of HavaTampa Jewels, will you? Just ask Charlie to put them on my account. And, don't you boys go and smoke one, y'hear? It'll stunt your growth, just like chewing tobacco, such as that Bull of the Woods I found stashed away under the back porch steps. Neither of you have any idea how it got there, now do you?"

"Shoot no, Daddy Dean."

"Helloooooo, Mr. Bird! Good morning to you and we were wondering when Mrs. Bird would be coming by again with her delicious lemon cake?

We finish supper and were now out in the yard catching lightning bugs in our Ball jars on this sweltering summer evening. The temperature surely would drop sometime, but now wasn't the time as our parents sat on the porch cooling themselves by waving the small bamboo hand fans sponsored, on one side, by the First Baptist Church, and Western Auto on the other. "You boys come on in now. It's time to hit the sack so you can get a good night's sleep for tomorrow. This is the third time I've called you, so get in here right this minute, young men!"

Before you could count to ten, we were fast asleep ready for the coming day with the milkman, the customers, and the last stop at the bakery for goodies. Only the sounds of the night could be heard, and they were generally the chorus of crickets echoing through the nocturnal silence joined by an occasional cry from some barn owl, or the screeching of bats soaring through the trees.

Morning came quickly and we were up and ready to board that milk truck as we waited on the front porch steps for Mr. Presley to round the corner and stop in front of our house. The sky was pitch black and only the front light of the Cheatam's house shone through the trees that softly illuminated the surrounding bushes and telephone poles. After a few minutes we could barely hear the sound of gears grinding as the lone motor vehicle turns down Hart Avenue and headed west on our street. We spotted Mr. Presley behind the wheel of his beat-up, not-so-shiny-new, sort of white truck. "Mornin'', Mr. Presley, we're ready to go."

"Hop on board, boys, and I'm glad to have you helping out. Let's get going so I can keep on schedule." Panky, you stand here and, Rego, you stand in the door and hold onto that handle so you won't go out the door when I make a hard left turn. First stop is up here at the Williams', and they get two quarts of homogenized milk plus one carton of eggs. Rego, you grab the milk and eggs that Panky hands you, run down and deliver it, then pick up the empties and bring them back for Panky to store in back of the truck. Watch out, too, 'cause the roads are bumpy, and you're liable to bounce right off the truck before you know it, and wind up on the street face down on the concrete! I'd sure hate to have to explain that to Mrs. Dean."

'Round about 6:30 a.m. we had delivered most of the milk and sundry items as the lean, mean, milk- delivering machine approached the service entry at the rear of Zeb's Bakery. We could smell those donuts cooking and suddenly I was famished. The owner offered us as many of the hot glazed morsels as we could eat, and I could eat as many as he offers. Rego must have devoured eight and I wasn't far behind as Mr. Presley asked us to reboard for the short trip back to Granny's. We were stuffed! We were borderline sick! Another bump in the road and we would puke. Lordy, too much sugar, fat, milk, and cream for our overstretched puny little stomachs to assimilate at one time.

Rego says, "Panky, I've got some Bull of the Woods chewing tobacco for us to try today, and old man Presley won't care, do you think?"

"Shoot, I don't know but I'm willing to try some." I removed the cellophane wrapper from the dark brown rectangle and bit off one of the corners. It was gawd awful! Still, I couldn't let on to Rego and Mr. Presley that I didn't like the taste. I stuffed the plug way back in the far left corner of my mouth, next to the area where my wisdom teeth would someday appear.

Mr. Presley asked, "How is it, Panky? That Bull of the Woods is the best tobacco you can buy. Sure beats that Beach Nut loose-leaf style. Here, let me have a plug and I'll hand it right back to you."

Mr. Presley bit off a plug from the opposite corner where I had begun. Rego decided to pass and he said he wanted to think about it. The truth is he was chicken, and we knew it. Rego always had this way of goading people into something while he abstained. As we left the paved road we suddenly hit a series of ruts in the hard, clay soil as the milk truck bounced off the four wheels and landed sharply back down on the surface. I was airborne for about one second that seemed like an eternity, and the tobacco plug decided to exit my mouth and head down the old esophagus towards my tummy. Clunk! There it sat as I began to spit the remains out the door of the truck onto whatever got in the way. I began to feel real sick and woozy and my skin turned a pale shade of green.

"I can't wait for some more of those hot greasy donuts along with that rich creamy cold milk tomorrow," said Rego, and Mr. Presley agreed.

"Panky, you don't look so good, my boy. Did you go and swallow some of that tobacco that you was chewing? Lordy, that is enough to make most folks puke!"

"Can we go home now? I don't believe that I was cut out for chewing tobacco. I'm just going to lay down on the floor in the back of the truck, if you don't mind, Mr. Presley."

"Panky, go and get a big drink of water, and that'll make you feel lots better," as Mr. Presley let out this huge laugh. "Okay, boy, but you'd better not let on what happened when Mrs. Dean sees you, or she'll switch your butt for sure."

Soon after we arrived back at Ida Avenue, and Granny's house, I was glad to see that Granny had a rush flower order, so she was out in the playhouse, as I casually walked into the bathroom, puked my lungs out, and staggered to the back porch for a nap.

Rego thought the entire ordeal was a riot and he couldn'y stop telling everyone at the pool.

Soon the lifeguards began to ask, "Hey, Panky, got a plug of Beach Nut over here. Want some?"

"Panky, heard where you're an old pro with Bull of the Woods. I got plenty of it for free, so you won't have to go and buy some. Here's a plug you can enjoy."

Are you crazy? You must have mistaken me for Rego. He's the one who got sick and puked. Isn't that true, Rue?"

"Panky, you're a lying sack of sheep shit!"

Myrtle Wright, Opp Municipal Pool, circa 1955

No One Could Dive Like Myrtle

The concrete rectilinear cavity was thirty feet across by one hundred feet in length. And, the depth varied from approximately two feet to twelve down at the drain. At the twelve foot end the high-dive structure sat ominously adjacent to the low board. The Opp Municipal Swimming Pool was the center of recreation during the sweltering summer days in south Alabama, and it's no wonder that the younguns waited impatiently for the coach to open the gate at nine o'clock every morning. Hell, where else could you get a Coke and a bag of Lays Barbecue Potato Chips for sweeping out the men's and women's locker rooms, and still enjoy a full day of swimming and running 'round the concrete in total defiance of the lifeguard's whistles?

At the deep end of this man-made ersatz pond were two wooden planks mounted on sturdy iron stanchions. One board was about three feet above pool level while the other board seemed to disappear into the clouds. The high dive was reserved for budding Ester Williams or crazy dare devils like Harry Jackson, Charles Nelson, or Louie Grimes. No telling how many belly flops resulted from the last minute panics and total disorientation as the divers became airborne, only split seconds away from the rock-hard, blue-green, chlorine-saturated cold water that siphoned down from the omnipresent Opp water tower - seen for 20 miles around the county.

We southerners are a visual people. Water tanks mask where you are. The bulbous gray monolith rises above the trees and low buildings and becomes the monument for high schools boys to utilize for significant rites of passage, such as hand-painted epithets. "Beat Kensington Eagles!" "Go Bobcats!" Beat those little fuckers on the football gridiron or my name painted here will be mud for another 365 days. Annual ritualistic misdemeanors, never enforced, surround the permanently embossed name of the town, followed by a comma, then the abbreviation of the state, like we don't really know where we are here in this county. A boldly painted OPP, AL alerts me to my arrival at Granny's.

The Opp Municipal Pool was situated amidst the park which contains a tennis court, the city water tank, a seesaw, a whirl around, several sets of swings that take us up to the stratosphere, and many large trees and bushes that provide cover whenever we need to hide, for one reason or another. The pool is the main attraction and it was sacrosanct. No one would dare to vandalize the pool or its facilities. Lordy knows, all there was to do was swim and sunbathe on many summer days, so why mess with a good thing. Besides, if someone caught you trespassing or vandalizing the pool or clubhouse facilities Coach Nolen would automatically suspend your pool privileges with absolutely no recourse for appeal. This is the word that had come forth, passed down through generations, and everyone simply abided by its meaning, or woe be unto you, brother.

Most important in the daily procedures were the hours of operation because the children plan their entire schedules around this time. If you know there is going to be a western movie at the Royal Theater, at 2:00 p.m., then you swim your butt off in the morning. If the matinee consists of some second-rate comedy then take it easy in the morning and continue with your swim, and frolic in afternoon. If the movie is "Sierra Sunrise" or "Susanna Pass," then count on missing your time at the pool after dinner. Let us bow our heads in prayer, chillun.

Roy Rogers Riders Club Pledge

1. *Be neat and clean.*

2. *Be courteous and polite.*

3. *Always obey your parents.*

4. *Protect the weak and help them.*

5. *Be brave but never take chances.*

6. *Study hard and learn all you can.*

7. *Be kind to animals and care for them.*

8. *Eat all your food and never waste any.*

9. *Love God and go to Sunday school regularly.*

10. *Always respect our flag and our country.*

In lower Alabama, that summer sky was a dull gray as cloud cover develops shortly after sunrise. And, the temperature hovers around ninety degrees, with the humidity close behind. The smell of ozone fills the air and we nourish that sensual effervescence along with the fragrances of gardenias, dogwood, and honeysuckle.

Everyday, Rego and I run from Granny's to the pool, from the pool back to Granny's for dinner, and back to the pool after our naps. We run just to have a fountain Coke, and to shop for Levi's at Leo's Economy Store. We run everywhere. Our bodies are finely hewn machines - sinewy, lean, mean or, just plain skinny. Not one ounce of fat camps out on our puny, frames.

We lived from September until June when school was out and the pool opened for the hot, sultry summer season. We wore faded, shredded Levis with the patches sewn over holes where our knees have worn through; and we eliminated any sign of footwear. The soles of our feet were like elephant hide impenetrable by most objects, notwithstanding rusty nails and broken glass, and the ensuing tetanus shots.

Because he was the absolute leader and arbitrator of all occurrences around the pool, Coach Nolen must be discussed, and analyzed. Here was a young man, truly southern, whose mission in life was to train young boys in the fine art of a contact sport known, in Dixie, as a para-religious experience practiced in the sanctuary of a coliseum on Saturday afternoon, or Friday evenings. You guessed it - football, southern style. Coach Nolen was the supreme commander of all football activities at Opp High School. The school was located on the north side of town, comprised of one hundred percent white students and one hundred percent white faculty. It was very small school compared to those in Mobile, Birmingham, or the Division One programs, up in Montgomery.

Coach couldn't wait for the opportunity to come each summer when he could take advantage of and mock my so-called Yankee accent. He said that I call him   "Coo - ach." Hell, he thought I sounded funny and I knew he was a true redneck with that Alabama drawl. This became ritualistic and I actually looked forward to arriving in Opp, and expecting this harassment from the Coach. It became part of the syntax of the summer. Coach Nolen was in charge of the pool and its facilities during the three months of operation, from June until the beginning of September. I'm certain that this task was one way of moonlighting to bolster his teaching and coaching income. In turn, all of the lifeguards reported to the Coach, and he was known as the person in charge.

Coach never suspected it but Rego and I knew how to manipulate him. Somewhere between the time the pool opened in the morning and the noon dinner we'd suffer from extreme hunger pangs as a result of all the swimming, and running, and swimming, and...you get the picture. Since we had no pocket change for snacks we conjure up ways to sucker Coach into some work for pay. Usually, he paid us the huge stipend of twenty-five cents for the menial tasks performed. That quarter, however, bought us two Cokes, and a bag of potato chips, just enough to hold us over until the noon whistle.

Coach Nolen held in his supreme command the nominations of several lifeguards during the summer months. I was never a serious contender for one of these positions because Coach perceived my physique as being similar to that of a starving refugee. How could I possibly transport someone in danger to safety while swimming in the pool? He always underestimated my strength and my ability to react in a panic situation. More importantly, he underestimates my desire to wear the lifeguard's whistle, cap, and title. That is what really hurt

"Panky, I'll race you to the pool," Rego shouted across the dining room.

"Let's go, Rego," was my reply as we blasted out the front door and I am a mere three or four feet ahead of my cousin.

We are at full speed by the time we hit our stride in front of Miriam Donaldson's house next door. Streaks of sheer light speed with the grace of two gazelles running through fields of grain, our knees pulled high as our hamstrings became fully extended, racing across the intersection in order to beat the oncoming traffic. Sometimes, it was a '50 Chevy or a senior citizen on foot, or an old black man pulling the reigns of a horse drawn buckboard. Of course, this is an illusion. In fact, we run like two Mexican jumping beans. With two blocks to go we blazed in a dead heat past the First Methodist Church, down past the empty tennis court, by the seldom occupied swing sets and now, the last seventy-five yards, it was all downhill through the trees and shrubs to the pool gate.

"Rego, last one to the gate is Harold's boyfriend."

That is all it took for Rego, the slower runner, to gain a final burst of speed held in reserve that would be crucial to the outcome of this foot race. Regardless of the adrenaline or of any supernatural ability I usually won that daily race. Reason? I run because of sheer terror because I am a small kid and, furthermore, the stakes are high. I might even have to kiss Harold, God forbid! (We consider Harold the town sissy.)

"OK Panky, you win. But, I ain't gonna kiss Harold. Wanna Dr. Pepper or a Coke?"

"Dr. Pepper'll be just fine, Rue, if I can ever catch my breath. You almost beat me this time so I'll give you less of a head start from now on, boy."

"Rego, Panky, get your butts in here, settle down and behave," said Coach Nolen, and he means it.

"Coach, how's about a couple of quarters to clean up the locker rooms and sweep 'round the pool?"

"Okay, you two, but make darn sure the women's locker room is clear before you burst in there, like you did the other day. One of these days you're going to walk in there, and Miriam Donaldson's going to come out and kick your butts!" Miriam lived next door to Granny and Daddy Dean and she was a teenager when we were pipsqueaks.

Heck, that was the only way we can get a shot of a little tittie, and that never hurt any young boy, for Pete's sake! One of our victims was Myrtle Wright who tattled on us, and she said she would tell our parents if we ever did that to her again. Myrtle was my heartthrob, and I am very sensitive to how she feels about me. I wouldn't do a thing to upset her, and so Rego and I made sure Myrtle wasn't present when we acted up.

Boy, could Myrtle dive off that high board and she had perfect form, almost every time. I idolized her ability to do a jack knife, or a swan, or a full gainer when I could barely keep my legs and feet together for the most basic of any dive. "Hey Rue, and Butch, let's sit over here and watch Myrtle practice off the high dive. She says she's going to try a half gainer and I'll believe it when I see it."

So, the three of us placed our little frames on the bench adjacent to the life guard stand and proceeded to watch Myrtle scale the ladder clear up ten feet. Just watching her wiggle that little butt of hers as she climbed up those stairs was enough to make my day. *My hormones were racing at a tender age.* Feet together, hands down by her sides, eyes straight ahead, she began her approach down the board. She sprang up for the last jump to gain the altitude necessary to get her legs and feet up perpendicular-out in front. Then, with those feet tucked together, toes pointed, she reached for her toes, holds her position for a split second and then threw her head and upper body back to form a straight perpendicular to the waterline-line. Myrtle's hands, head, torso and legs entered the pool with nary a splash. "10, 10, 10," we shouted as she swam over to our side of the pool. "That's a perfect dive, Myrtle, how come we can't dive like you? Come in to the clubhouse and we'll buy you a Dr. Pepper and some barbecue potato chips."

About this time Harry Jackson, the senior lifeguard, came over to us as we were sitting at the deep end dangling our legs in the water, sat down beside us and said, " You boys know how to keep from getting the clap? Well, let me tell you."

I looked at Rego and he looked at me and we both wondered, "What in the heck is the clap?"

Harry said, "When you're through you pee. That's what gets rid of the bug that gives you the clap."

What in the heck does this have to do with Myrtle diving off the high board, we wondered?

"Rego, have you, Butch, and Panky been uptown to see the tinker selling all sorts of stuff?" said the Coach. "He's got pots and pans, animals and snakes that you should see. He usually rambles through these parts every summer and we like to think of him as an institution here in Opp. A little weird but he's okay."

"Rego, let's quit swimming and hightail it up there before dinner, okay?"

"All right with me, Panky, but we don't have our money from Coach yet. Coach, can you pay us in advance for sweeping out the locker rooms, plus a couple of extra quarters? We'll pay you back this afternoon."

"Here's some change, you two, and I'd better see a return of my investment or it'll come out of your hides," was Coach's reply.

Shortly before noon we changed back into our jeans and then we ran up the street towards the post office where this vagabond had his wooden wagon, sort of like the sheep wagon you'd see in the western movies, with all of his paraphernalia displayed. What a character he was - scrubby, with a beard and tattered clothes, but his sales pitch was eloquent. Here was a natural born salesman with that critical ability of creating a need within everyone within earshot and being able to negotiate the correct sales price for whatever goods or animals being considered by the townsfolk. This tinker had rabbits, foxes, squirrels, pots, pans, clothing, herbs and snakes. Snakes!

Rego, Butch and I literally went crazy when we spied the slithery creatures in their makeshift cages, and we simply had to have one. Our pulses accelerated and when the tinker opened the cage and gathered this small reptile we couldn't believe our eyes. This vine snake is about a foot long, a quarter inch in diameter, and couldn't hurt a flea. Well, maybe a flea but nothing else would fit down its measly mouth. Other that the fact that it moved the most significant characteristic of the snake was the color. On its back the color was a bright Irish green and its belly was a softer, more yellow-green. It was the cutest "thang" I'd ever seen.

"Hey boys, hold this one for a while. Won't hurt you. Get familiar and you won't be afraid. Put it around your neck and feel it move," said the tinker.

I reply, "Are you out of your mind?" I am terrified at the thought of this thing creeping 'round my body.

Rego says, "Panky, put it 'round your neck and I'll do it too."

Rego always maked me go first and, like a dummy, I did. "Say, it feels weird but not too bad. Tickles and its a strange sensation but, otherwise, I don't mind." Knowing that this was totally strange and unlike anything we'd ever done before we got a wild charge out of it, like we were getting away with something."

"Panky, bet you won't wear that snake around you neck when you go home for dinner, just to scare your folks," Butch challenges us.

"Bet I will too, Butch. I'll wear it and Rego gets to ring the doorbell. When they answer they won't know what's happening until they stare at my neck and see the snake begin to slither."

"Mister, how much do you want for the snake?," we asked.

"Gimme fifty cents and he's all yours. It eats insects and small leaves, so don't go feeding him grits, and stuff like that."

We gave the tinker everything we had, and then proceed to giggle all the way home. Butch went on down to his house and said he'd join us back at the pool later. As we approach Granny's house we stopped to regain our composure, as if we had any to begin with. I coiled the snake around my neck and then proceeded to put on my poker face. Rego and I slowly and quietly walked up the front porch steps when we heard everyone inside the house preparing for the noon dinner. Rego reached up to turn the mechanical doorbell as I stepped squarely in the middle of the front door, with our friend slithering from my shoulders up to my ears.

Our mothers, Lucy and Evelyn, opened the door and said, "What are you two doing now? You never ring the doorbell. Why are you standing in that doorway with those silly grins on your faces? You talk to us, young men. And, what is that thing around your neck, Panky? Granny, come here and look at how strange these two are acting."

At this point the two of them recognized the object around my neck, and their perfectly lipsticked mouths begin to let out screams that could pierce a steel reinforced concrete bunker. These damsels came apart at the seams. Neighbor's doors flew open, cats scurried up the trees, the hens in the backyard flew the coup, and Rego and I fell down laughing. We were choking to death and our stomachs cramped from the strain of our own laughter. It was a marathon of comedy and, by far, the liveliest event to occur on Ida Avenue since a young and well-endowed Miriam Donaldson walked out to retrieve her morning newspaper clad in a very short negligee. Rego and I'll never forget that sight. Think that was the point in our physiological development when we began to feel some serious hormonal changes.

Mom and Aunt Evelyn almost had to be taken to the Mizell Memorial Hospital, and Granny to the couch for respiration, because of our prank. Rego and I assured them that the snake was harmless and we found a glass Ball jar in the kitchen so our little buddy could have a home. Throughout our noon meal Rego and I couldn't keep straight faces. We'd take a few bites of food and then burst into laughter. This pattern was repeated about a dozen times before we were warned that one more outburst would result in a serious switching. This threat settled us down for about five seconds. There was absolutely no hesitation in my mother's and Aunt Evelyn's voices when they emphatically say, "The snake WILL be returned now to that tinker for a full refund, or else."

Do you think that Rego or I questioned the "or else" for one, single minute? We did not. Discretion dictated that we capitulate and get uptown quickly to return our newly acquired friend.

Laughing all the way up Ida Avenue across the empty lot and up to the post office we rehearse what we would say to the tinker. "Sir, our mothers said we can't keep the snake, so can we have our money back?"

"Boys, I don't want a used snake. How can I make a living if everyone returns what they bought? Tell you what. I'll take it back but it'll cost you a quarter for my troubles, so you get only a quarter back. Fair enough?"

It's all right with me, Panky," Rego said.

"Okay Rego, let's get our money back and beat feet back to the pool."

We reluctantly surrendered the snake to the tinker in return for half our investment. Obviously, he was miffed with our return but he made fifty percent on the deal so he could resell the little fella to other idiots, like us. Soon, we left the post office to headed back to the pool but not before stopping at Dean's Pharmacy for a fountain Coke. Nothing, absolutely nothing beat the taste of a fountain Coke along with one of Delia Barganier's chicken salad sandwiches, which were stocked fresh daily on a plate situated atop the fountain. These delicacies consisted of fresh chicken salad spread on Holsum bread, with the crust removed, and then wrapped in Cut Rite wax paper to preserve the flavor. Delia was Granny's sister-in-law who lived next door to us, and this was one way that Delia picks up some extra change.

Next stop was Uncle Johnny's store, right next door to the pharmacy. We loved going into his store and teasing Rego with slogans such as, "See Rue for shoes," or "Rego Rue has holes in his shoes," or "I'm Rego Rue. My dog, Buster, and I live in there too." Silly stuff, but fun. Most of all we want to use Uncle Johnny's shoe X-ray machine to view our feet under the green light, and use the pointer to measure our big and little toes. Uncle Johnny yelled over for us to curtail this activity because he had paying customers who needed to be fitted for shoes. And, our feet were filthy and probably crawling with microscopic creatures just waiting to jump off into his machine.

When we returned to the pool and told Coach Nolen and the lifeguards about our purchase, and the terror that ensued, they couldn't stop laughing. As a matter of fact, they thought it was the funniest thing they've heard in a long time, and their only regret was not being present to witness the hysteria, first hand. Coach said, "Panky and Rego, you're darn lucky that your mothers didn't break your necks after that silly stunt. Maybe your fathers will take care of that personally, knowing them. Nonetheless, it is quite a tale and you two never cease to amaze me with your antics. By the way, go ahead and keep the quarter as good luck. I'll work it out of your hides tomorrow."

So, back to Myrtle and her diving. A much more gentile way to enjoy our leisure afternoons at the pool. First, she performed a beautiful side jack knife, then another half gainer, followed by an Ester Williams type swan dive. Shoot, I couldn't follow this act so around back of the clubhouse for some smokes. Is Coach here or has he gone home for lunch?

Who's got the Pall Malls?

My All Time Hero 'sides Roy, Dale and Gene

was Straight Arrow!

Blue Ribbions I won at Camp Grist, circa 1950

The Whampus Cat and Other Chuckles

"OK boys, tomorrow, bright and early, we leave for Camp Grist. All of your clothes have been marked and tagged with your names. Do you think you'll need anymore underwear, or are there laundry facilities up there?"

"Heck, I don't know, Mom, why don't you just put a couple extra pairs in our bags anyway? Rego, can you hardly wait or what? Have you ever been to camp, or is this your first time too?"

"No, Panky, I've known some kids here in Opp, who went last summer but this'll be my first time, just like you, and I can't wait. We are going to have a whole bunch of fun up there. Some of my buddies told me about the Girl Scout camp across the lake from us and that they raided the girls late at night by stealing the canoes and paddling over in the middle of the night."

"I wonder how long we'll be there. Mom, how long does camp last?"

My mother, Lucy, replied, "Seven days total and I'm sure you two won't miss us for one single minute."

Rego and I looked at one another, grinned, chuckled, and silently left the room before we uttered a reply. Silence in this case was golden. I think I remember running out the front door and tackling Rego right into the pampas grass bush. If our moms only knew the actual degree of excitement we felt they assuredly would have canceled our plans and kept a very close eye on our activities for the remainder of the summer vacation.

We woke the following morning at the crack of dawn because of our restless night's sleep. Our duffel bags were packed. We were dressed. We said good-bye to Granny and Daddy Dean, we had reserved our seats in the back of the station wagon, and, now, we were ready to get the show on the road. This summer was a first. First, in our annals of freedom from home for seven, whole days. Seven days off with the fellows and totally new adventures, and all of it without our parents' presence so we could barely control our emotions. As a matter of fact, we couldn't. We were two, nervous wrecks - two jumping beans trying to remain still in the back of the car. This was not going to be an easy task and we knew that Selma, AL was about two hours away from Opp; and the camp was another half hour out of Selma, up on a hill.

The four of us - Mom, Aunt Evelyn, Rego, and I - packed into Evelyn's station wagon, which was a Chevy woody and painted egg shell blue as I remember, to head up the road through Brantley, stopped at Highland Home for breakfast at Jack's was a treat for us. The only way folks from out of this area ever'd know that Highland Home existed is someone either referred to the tiny hamlet, or they had stopped at Jack's during a previous trip. Highland Home isn't even included on some road maps. As a matter of fact I recently tried to locate this town in my

Rand McNally's atlas, but no such luck. In addition to the public school that was set back a few hundred feet from the highway there were only a couple of other buildings, one of which was the Esso station - home of Jack's Cafe. This had been a regular stopover point for many folks between Montgomery and points down this way for the Saturday shopping exodus. That Esso station was the typical white stucco, one story, with the corner of the building constructed from art deco glass bricks and, at one end of the building, was Jack's. This "Main Street Style" of architecture was prominent durin' the fifties, and has recently come back into vogue. And, the decor inside the cafe was rather plain, with linoleum floor, several plastic laminate-topped tables, and the counter provided seats for approximately ten customers. But it was the marvelous aroma of homemade sausage and sugar-cured bacon on the grill that truly aroused the senses especially after a long drive. Those biscuits were freshly made from scratch, the grits weren't runny, the eggs practically chuckled, the milk pasteurized, but not homogenized, so the cream sat on top in your glass. And the freshly brewed coffee kept our parents asking for more servings. To the best of my recollection, Jack's Cafe still exists in the '90's, and so it should . . . simple food for a reasonable fare served up by good ol' country folk.

On the road again towards Selma, and Camp Grist as we witnessed one small wide spot in the road after another, town after town, until we reached the city limits of Selma. Needless to say, our mothers never stopped to inquire about directions, so we spent another half hour riding around in the back seat as they tried to obtain directions out of town and up the hill to the camp. At last, we found the dirt road which was your typical Alabama red clay that eventually found its way through the pine trees, up the hill, round the bend to Camp Grist. Rego and I bolted from the rear of the station wagon, raced up to the main building to meet other boys and Mr. Grist. Yes there really was individual named Grist and he was a man's man. . . tall, handsome, with a pure white head of hair cut in the flattop style. Rego and I introduced ourselves, told Mr. Grist the names of our hometowns and, last but not least, introduced our mothers as a matter of southern courtesy. Mr. Grist advised our parents to come back in seven days around dinnertime so that they could take us home. He also advised our parents that church services would be held on Sunday, and for them not to worry about the logistics of our religious persuasions. Indeed, we would go to Catholic or Protestant services under his guidance. Being a Catholic I was sorely disappointed because I thought this camp was a definite escape from the Sunday rituals observed at least fifty-two times a years, in addition to the Holy Days of Obligation. No matter how hard I tried the monkey called Catholicism made a permanent home on my back.

Our mothers then helped us to unload our duffel bags as they delivered last minute instructions as well as some spending money. Then came the flurry of hugs and kisses right in front of our peers. Yuk! I suppose this was necessary for their peace of mind but it always embarrassed Rego and me

Finally, Lucy and Evelyn hopped back into the Chevy as they probably whispered under their breaths, "Thank heavens, we're free for seven glorious days and I think we should really take advantage of it. Why don't we all go down the coast for a few days. I'm certain that Hank and Johnny will be ready in a heartbeat."

"Evelyn, I thought you'd never ask. Hank will want a few days away from Granny I can assure you. Let's get a move on as soon as we hit Opp. What is the name of that cute hotel in Ft. Walton Beach, the one with the cabins in back? You know the one I'm talking about but I can't remember the name."

"Lucy, I don't care where we stay as long as it's as far away from Granny as possible."

Rego and I gathered along with the throngs of other boys as the counselors read the cabin assignments and we were assigned the Cabin B Team. Each of these rustic wooden cabins housed eight lads, plus one counselor. "Panky, I'll flip you for the top bunk, and I call tails."

"Okay, Rue, let me get this quarter out of my jeans and we'll just see who's sleeping up or down. You called tails, and tails it is. Shucks, I lose again for the five thousandth time."

Rego beat me at almost everything in life and you will see how this trend changes as our lives evolve.

Soon, the remainder of our cabin mates filtered in and chose their bunks and began to store their belongings. We all introduced ourselves and discovered that, for the most part, we all hailed from similar small towns scattered throughout Alabama, with few exceptions such as Mobile, Birmingham, Mobile, or Huntsville. In the relative quiet a much larger and slightly older fellow jaunted through the door and introduced himself as our cabin counselor. He said he was from Phenix City, and that he was our guiding light for the next seven days. This rather young and semi-tough drill instructor type asked, "Does anyone here have cigarettes, chewin' tobacco, or liquor in their bags? I'll take it now if you do because if Mr. Grist discovers where you are holding back he will call your parents immediately, and you'll be outta here, just like that. I know you're too young to buy any beer so I assume there ain't any stored away."

Our reply, in unison, was, "No Bull of the Woods in this group, sir." And that translates into no tobacco with these troops.

In these camps described in the back pages of Boy's Life there are photographs of beautiful log cabin style buildings with forest green awnings. These buildings are surrounded by tall pine trees for as far as you can see, and the buildings are located on the shore of a magnificent, deep blue alpine lake. And, the boys in the photographs are all attired in clean, white tee shirts embossed with the camp logo on the chest, and their moccasins are worn with perfectly clean white socks pulled up over their calves. These young lads, in addition, possess ersatz Third

Reich Young folk smiles glued on their freckled faces. Indeed, these images were not, repeat not, Camp Grist. Camp Grist was ever so slightly different in that our primary building resembled a fire station. The pine trees were juxtaposed with scrub oaks and laurel and the lake was down the hill out of view and resembled more of a large, slightly muddy pond. Our facilities were, indeed, that of the YMCA ilk and our brochure that was mailed to entice boys to attend was printed in black and white with a small photo or two of the amphitheater, rifle range, canoes and, of course, our gleaming Mr. Grist. No clean white tee shirts and kids with toothy smiles screwing up our image here folks! This was summer boot camp, 'Bama style. To us, however, the camp was paradise because we were away from home, the dominance of our parents and the teasing of our sisters for a whole week. What trouble could we get into now? That was the sixty-four thousand dollar question. And, we were determined to find the answer(s).

I might add that there wasn't a black child to be seen anywhere. Alabama was segregated not only in philosophies but also in facilities. Hence, no white boys at black camps and vice versa. Somehow I felt that not very many camps catered to black boys in Alabama, in the '50s. Since I had lived in northern and western towns the thought of attending school, or camp for that matter, with boys and girls of different colors and nationalities did not bother me. I never understood segregation then, and I still don't today, especially regarding children.

The supper hour approached so we walked over towards the dining hall only to pass by our community bathroom. This small building was our only facility for showering and for other obvious biological requirements. Adequate, but not very pristine. It would do, and since we had absolutely no intention of maintaining hygiene, the showers really were of little concern to most of us. You know what I liked about the whole camp? The rustic buildings, the red clay soil that inched its way right up to the bases of the pine trees, the trails that led in all directions to the places where our activities were scheduled, and the friendliness of most of the boys. If the camp were constructed today the buildings, in all probability, would be constructed from stucco, with tile roofs, and there would be a distinct addition of concrete paths, patios and other unnecessary physical plant. Instead, Camp Grist was exactly as it should be - slightly remote and rustic and warm in spirit.

"Rue, what do you suppose we'll have for supper; and I wonder how late we can stay up?" I was always interested in the next meal as if it was the biblical last supper, and what would lie ahead in the wee hours long after our counselors had retired for the evening.

"Lordy, Panky, it had better taste like Gladdy Mae's cooking or else we're in for a long week here at camp. To tell you the truth, Miller, I'm so excited that I won't be able to eat for a while anyway. I've dreamed about going away to camp so being here is almost too good to be true. You know what I want to learn while we're here? How to braid those lanyards the lifeguards use to hang their metal whistles around their necks. I don't know how to braid and the counselors teach you in classes. Trouble is what colors do I want in my lanyard? Shucks, don't matter long as it looks good."

During supper, which I remember as being palatable, we were introduced and given a short speech by the larger-than-life, gleaming Ipana-like smile, white-flat-topped Mr. Grist. This man towered above most of us pip-squeaks, and his voice rang true throughout the dining hall. The crux of his talk was about discipline and that our respective cabin counselors had control of our lives for the next seven days mainly because they had our balls in their hands. If we stepped out of line the counselors were to squeeze our family jewels as hard as they could. Mr. Grist got my immediate attention and held it for the greater part of the next seven days. I couldn't think of anything that would accomplish this objective and be more threatening to a group of preadolescents than his most informative speech.

Later that evening the full contingency of campers and counselors gathered down at the amphitheater, which was located a few hundred feet from the dining hall, under the tall, fragrant pines.

Lordy, the smell of the pine needles was something I'll never forget and, to this day, I consider being one of the favorite sensations of my olfactory nerve.

Now, the purpose of this gathering was to determine the daily schedules for our various cabin assignments. The counselors took to the stage and began to read aloud. "Boys assigned to Cabin A report to the rifle range at 8:30 in the morning. Cabin C, you report to the archery range at 8:30. Cabin B, you'll be meeting up next to the small shop to learn lanyard weaving, also at 8:30." And, so on. What we were all dying to hear, however, weren't these schedules but were the swimming schedule.

Swimming was the daily event that Rego and I looked forward to the most and I'm certain that our love of the liquid stuff was highly instigated by the countless hours we'd spent at the Opp Municipal Pool. Suddenly, the counselor announced when we were to be unleashed and the mayhem would begin at 10:00 in the morning until 11:30, and from 2:00 until 4:00 in the afternoon everyday, unless it rained. Could we be happier than two pigs in a poke? Twice a day we could revert back to a Darwin-like existence in the eternal quest of those dreaded maladies known as "pink eye", ear infections, stomach cramps, sunburn and physical exhaustion. I almost started shaking with excitement and I don't believe that I had ever swum in a lake before. Ever! Been to the Gulf of Mexico, Atlantic Ocean, many municipal pools but never a huge, deep mountain lake. All I could think of was Tarzan and how he swung down the vines, through the trees, to drop into that quintessential river or lake, only to discover other beings who occupied the same area - like crocodiles, hippos, piranhas, or other creatures that could kill little kids. Shit! Better think twice before running down that hill to the lake and diving into a totally unknown entity. I knew we didn't have those pending threats to our survival in this lake but I still thought that somehow I would be Tarzan, or another wild hero, who would conquer this vast body of uncharted water.

"Lights out, lights out," echoed throughout the camp. The counselors, almost in unison, issued this edict and, even though it was relatively early we were physically exhausted, and ready for sleep. Our minds traveled at 100 miles per hour, so we couldn't possibly slow down long enough for the fatigue to conquer our mental and physical state. As we prepared for our first night's sleep our counselor told us that, after lights out, we would hear a spooky story every night while we were at camp. With that in mind the group in Cabin Bravo took all of about thirty seconds to undress and to jump into our respective bunks. Door shut, lights out, and all you could hear was the rustling of the trees, an occasional whippoorwill, or an owl hooting in the sultry night air. The tension mounted as we awaited the first of many ghost stories that were guaranteed to curdle our blood!

"Tonight, lads, we will introduce y'all to The Whampus Cat, the scariest creature to come down the hill by our lake and wander up to our cabins here at Camp Grist," so said our counselor in a trembling voice designed to literally scare the living shit out of us.

I lay there totally spellbound with my eyes opened as wide as possible. The counselor literally kept us spellbound as we followed him through this tale of terror and the supernatural, and of the possibility that the Whampus Cat could stray into our cabin looking for a meal consisting of young, tender, white males. My nerves were tingling and I couldn't get to sleep for at least twenty to thirty seconds after the conclusion of the story; and I wonder if the beans and franks we ate for supper had anything to do with the recurring nightmares of a carnivorous cat that attacked little boys throughout the night?

"Hit the deck, lads, time to rise and shine. Get out of those bunks and straighten them up. Rego, sweep the floor and Harry, empty the trash can. Let's get finished so we can beat the other cabins to the showers, and still be first for breakfast. We're having flapjacks and bacon, and today I'm real hungry. Everyone be at breakfast by seven thirty."

The group in Cabin Bravo performed like a rocket shot from a canon. In all of about thirty seconds we were dressed, crew cut hair combed with the use of our hands, and chores completed. The usual race began to the showers and then to the dining hall. If one were to take an aerial photo of the ground that image would probably resemble an ant farm, scurrying in every which direction, moving in a totally irrational pattern, and getting nowhere fast. The sum total of our energies would have been sufficient to launch man to the moon. It was total madness, and all this consuming of energy made it possible for us to retire early in the evening without much hesitation or reservation.

After breakfast Rego said, "Panky, I feel sick. Boy, do I have to go dookie, so wait for me here and I'll be back shortly."

Dookie is a southern euphemism meaning human defecation. Need I say more?

Rego didn't look good. He was pale and complained of chills. Then, he made a mad dash for the community bathroom, so I knew he was in real bad shape. After a half hour I figured that it was no use waiting around, so I reported to the rifle range. This area of the camp was situated in a remote part because god only knows where the bullets would fly once those rifles were aimed by preteen, city slicker, snot-nosed brats, some of whom never fired a gun in their lives. I knew that I'd win the rifle competition because of my prowess and expertise learned while listening to the Hashknife Hartley, Straight Arrow, and Roy Rogers radio shows. My aim was keen and my hand, as steady as a rock. But, we weren't handed pearly handled, silver engraved Colts. We were given twenty-two caliber rifles! Holding a rifle was entirely different. It was placed high on your shoulder and the stock adjacent to your chin. The barrel had a sight down on the end which must be aligned with the rear sight above the chamber in order to be aimed correctly. Furthermore, the rifle shot real bullets! My adrenalin was starting to flow, like Niagara Falls, and my confidence was waning rapidly.

As I sat there on the bench waiting for my turn to fire the rifle a counselor yelled "Panky, move fast, there's a snake under your feet." I sprang up about six feet (should have won the high jump ribbon then and there) and watched this object slither in the area of the sand where my feet had just rested. The counselor took my rifle and he fired six rapid rounds into and around that snake as we all watched in horror. I mean, really! This little guy was pumped full of holes, deader than a doornail. Sure, I was scarred, but so was the little snake. The counselor indicated that this was a poisonous snake called a moccasin which was indigenous to this area. We were all previously briefed by our counselors that poisonous reptiles were omens of the devil, but not the non-poisonous species, such as the indigo or vine snakes. I ask you. How were these little buggers to know if they were good or bad?

A few minutes later after I stopped trembling we settled back down to business and then it was my turn on the rifle range. Ask me how I performed. Better yet, please don't because my ego was bruised and a city kid, from Baltimore, could have better scores than this humbled sharpshooter. Pitiful, pitiful scores at only fifty yards. A sorry excuse for a country kid. Well, I wasn't really a country kid. Even though I had lived mostly in suburban areas of large cities I was Huckleberry Finn or Tom Sawyer at heart. I always considered myself to have a dead aim with a firearm. This time, however my nerves had been rattled not by a rattler, but by a moccasin. Tomorrow was another day, however, and I still had the rest of time at camp to redeem myself. But today remained a disaster.

Rego still hadn't appeared on the scene and I never gave it a second thought. Perhaps he had decided to braid lanyards or something else that kept him close to the bathroom. After the rifle competition was completed, we walked back to check in the rifles and ammunition. Our counselor walked up to advise me that Rego was back at the cabin with the "scoots." He was in sad shape and that it looked like the flu or something else that would ruin his stay. Later that day, we began our marathon melee down to the lake to swim, splash, wrestle, and to dive from the floating pier until our legs were virtually unable to support our meager torsos. Where was Rego? Still back up the hill saying "hello" to the commode. When the lifeguard blew the final whistle we began our run back up the hill to prepare for other camp activities, and to have supper. That run back up the hill never seemed as much fun nor did we reach lightnin' speed as the bolt down not because of the natural laws of gravity but because of the synergy caused by young boys' attraction to water molecules. I returned to our cabin to discover that Rego was one, sick kid. He had visited the camp nurse and the diagnosis was the Camp Grist flu. So much for the remainder of Rego's time at camp. While the rest of us were running, shooting, eating, swimming, braiding, weaving, reading, old Rego was performing his own four-event marathon consisting of running, sitting, crapping, and puking!

A couple of days passed by as I managed to pick up several first places in three track and field events. If my memory serves me correctly the events in which I excelled were the fifty-yard dash, the high jump (surely from previous experience at the rifle range), and the broad jump. The truth is the primary reasons for my awards were the absence of Rego, my toughest competitor. Had he been fit I might have settled for second place in one or more events. The fact remains, however, that I was the undisputed champion in the Camp Grist Olympic Games Track and Field, and the awards would be distributed during the last night's ceremonies. This was worth the trip to camp alone, because winning these events made me feel like a million dollars. I was always the runt, the skinny kid, the one who was always passed over for selection on the football or baseball team, the one who couldn't compete with his peers, or so I thought. These victories proved that not all kids were created equal, and that I actually ruled supreme in those track and field events.

I took those blue ribbons home that summer and my mother placed them in a safe spot - for about forty years. Just this past fall she returned them along with several other bits of memorabilia for my scrapbook.

Rego confined his diet to clear liquids, mostly 7 Up and soups. My oh my, this boy was sick of this restrictive intake, but then again, Rue was just plain sick. About the only time we would see him was in his bunk back in Cabin Bravo at the end of the day. The third or fourth night, as we were preparing to hit the sack, our counselor warned us of the impending horror tale that created heart attacks even among youngin's. This tale was about "Von Doom and the Blue-Gummed Niggers," the most frightening tale of all times! And, this was an understatement as he began to describe the monster in Dickensonian terms. This creature ate children, wild and domestic animals - everything in its path - after cooking them in a cauldron of boiling oil! Can you imagine Rego hearing this on top of a bad stomach? We all knew that his sleep would be interrupted with races to the bathroom, several hundred feet away from our cabin. This left plenty of opportunities for Von Doom to snatch Rego from under our noses and carry him off for the fate that none of us could comprehend.

Speaking of deep sleep, mine was suddenly interrupted by a screaming boy sitting on top of me while he was yelling, "Where's my tool box, where's my tool box?" His hands were tight around my throat and the air had been squeezed from my lungs. Couldn't scream. Couldn't breath. I was helpless and scared shitless. My eyes bulged out of their sockets and I thought this was it. By this time, the counselor jumped out of his bunk, ran over, and grabbed Rego.

"Rego, what you doing boy? Wake up. You're having a nightmare."

"I'm all right now. Must have been a nightmare. Sorry, Panky, I thought you were stealing my toolbox. The one I had in Bryn Mawr, when we were younger. Hope I didn't hurt you."

"That's okay, Rego, I'm not hurt. But you sure scared hell out of me and, soon as I stop shaking, I'm goin' back to sleep." All of our cabin mates were wide-awake and cracking up with laughter. This hysteria lasted for about an hour and I giggled throughout the night and for most of the following day. Rego never did make it through the night without bolting from our cabin and breaking land speed records to the bathroom. Served him right. This toolbox must have been something really special for him to carry its memory as his personal luggage for many years. How dare he accuse me of the perpetrator of this felonious theft? For years we have laughed about this incident, and one of these days, I'm going to buy Rego a special toolbox of his very own.

Next morning, while we were having breakfast, Mr. Grist approached our table in the great dining hall and said, "Aren't you Panky Miller, from Opp? I hear you play the piano. Is that correct?"

A lump formed in my throat as I said very softly, "Yes sir, but I don't play very well."

"That's not what I hear, young man. We're having a skit during our last night's ceremonies and you have been elected to play and dress like Al Jolsen. Please report down to the stage at the amphitheater to try out the piano and your costume. We should have a great show for the camp, and I'm personally looking forward to hearing you play that piano."

I tried to finish my supper while the knot in my stomach grew larger. Lord God almighty! This was big time entertainment and my only previous audiences had been little old ladies who attended piano recitals on Sunday afternoons out of sheer boredom. Now, I was on the block. Not only did I have to play the piano in front of hundreds of my peers but, in addition, I had to don this ridiculous costume and paint my face black. In terms of pressure and anxiety this performance was on the same level as auditioning for a movie or a musical on Broadway. How did I get roped into playing for this event? Did Rego spill the beans? Was he trying to get even with me? Was this his way of settling the score because of his illness and my blue ribbon performances?

Perhaps this is one of Rego's best-kept secrets through the years and we'll possibly learn of its outcome only moments before he is laid to rest. Nonetheless, I was going to have a most humiliating experience, one that would promote a thousand laughs from the "peanut gallery" as I attempted to complete several boogie woogie tunes - error free - and look like Al Jolsen at the same time. Suddenly, I began to sweat bullets.

Well, psychiatrists indicate that whenever asked a question and your first response is "Well", it is an excuse to buy time. They are absolutely correct. The big day finally arrived and I reported to the back stage area for the final preparation with my costume and make-up. Putting on that black oily gook was loads of fun as my hands turned the same color. The came the white mouth. Another mess and the white make-up crept into the surrounding black creating an abstract version of what would best be described as the anal area of a zebra! We're talking major butterflies and these butterflies simply refused to fly in formation in my stomach and the thought of barfing was not out of the question.

Here you have literally everyone attending camp, the counselors, the kitchen help, Mr. Grist and Rego, sitting in the audience under the pines and the moonlight screaming and shouting at every person who ventured onto the stage. Some poor boys were selected to read poems while others were asked to sing a few camp songs that they were rehearsing for the very first time on stage only to be followed by Mr. Grist taking the microphone to say, "Now, we have as our last number Panky

Miller performing some Al Jolsen tunes on the piano. Panky is from Opp, and let's give him a big round of applause."

Applause? Sounded more like a few boys swatting fireflies in their hands as I walked onto the stage. My hands trembled and, thank God, I had a bench because my knees began to buckle out of sheer fright. I concentrated on the keys (which resembled my face - black/white and blurry) as my fingers blazed across the keys. Not a mistake and I was on fire! The musical notes and beat captured my audience as the boys began to clap in syncopated rhythm as my smile with the white greasy make-up grew larger and my eyes bulged out of their sockets. The final applause fell far short of deafening but the boys yelled for more. I had exhausted my repertoire so the gig was completed. I stood up, politely bowed, and repaired to back stage as I began to remove the gooey sticky black and white grease. Mr. Grist proceeded to walk onto the stage to thank those of us who performed and to make the final presentations and awards for this camp session.

Here sat Rego, probably for the first time in his life, with zero accomplishments to his credit for the week. Can you imagine his humiliation as those of us who won awards walked up to accept the first, second, and third prizes? I had won three blue ribbons in track and field.

"Panky, if I hadn't been sick you probably would not have won those blue ribbons."

My retort was, "That's just fine, Rue, but the fact remains I did and you didn't, so there. No doubt about it, though. You should have won first place blue ribbons for dookying, puking, and snoring!"

Next morning came all too quickly because this was the day when our parents arrived to retrieve us for the long drive home. We did everything possible in order to plan our getaway down the hill to escape from our parents. Car after car began to arrive from every conceivable county throughout Alabama, as the boys greeted their families in various ways - some tearful that camp was over, some happy to see their folks, some silent with the typical body language of boys, and then there were those who ran and hid - like Rego and me. Let's face it. We firmly believed our parents were simply going to drive for two hours from Opp, ask Mr. Grist our whereabouts, hear that we deserted camp, only for them to get back into the Woody and return to Opp, empty handed. Seemed like a good plan to us but, after hiding under our cabin for several minutes, we decided to capitulate and face the music.

"Rego, Panky, you get your tails out here this very minute. What do you think you're doing? Get your duffel bags, thank your counselor and Mr. Grist, say good-bye to your friends and get into this car. Now, get moving! You two look like you didn't bathe for a week. I know there are showers up here so I simply can't understand why you look like hoboes. Evelyn, do you notice a distinct odor in this car? Seems to me that we have a couple of piglets, not young men, for the long, hot ride home."

Roy Rogers Riders Club Prayer

Oh Lord, I reckon I'm not much just by myself.

I fail to do a lot of things I ought to do.

But Lord, when trails are steep and passes high,

Help me to ride it straight the whole way through.

And when in the falling dusk I get the final call,

I do not care how many flowers they send -

Above all else the happiest trail would be

For You to say to me, "Let's ride, my friend."

Amen

Roy and Trigger

D. C. To Dixie

The year was 1954 and I was in the 7th grade. My classmate, Chuck, and I had just completed our daily baseball practice out on the Bethesda Municipal Golf Course. We were very fortunate to have this monstrous open area only a few blocks from our houses, so the golf course became our playground for hours and hours everyday after school. This area backed up to the National Institute of Health, and there were zillions of new windows to break as we practiced our curve, fast, slider, knuckle and spit ball pitches until our arms were numb.

"Chuck, Panky is getting ready to have supper, so it's time for you to run along now."

"OK Mrs. Miller. I'll see you at school tomorrow, Panky."

Chuck was one of those kids you tolerated. He wasn't very nice. He didn't have many friends. He was basically a creep but a necessary creep in my life. Being a military kid moving from town to town every two or three years I needed all the instant buddies I could get. So, Chuck was a temporary friend. Chuck was about my size. . . small frame, blonde hair, sinewy, tough as nails, and insecure like me. He lived about a mile away in the typical eastern-colonial style house. Anyway, we were classmates and spent much time as a team reigning terror in the neighborhood and in school. We were always in detention hall. Always in trouble. Small insignificant trouble but still trouble as defined by the Papal archdiocese, in Washington, D.C.

To tell you what kind of a guy Chuck really was, he stole my one and only prized Rawlings baseball glove, scratched up the back, changed some of the lacing, and then had the audacity to say it was his glove that he bought it from some kid at Bethesda Chevy Chase Chase High. I never accused him to his face of stealing my glove. What kind of friend would steal his best friend's baseball glove? Only a total asshole.

After breakfast one morning my mother said, "How would you like to ride the bus down to Granny's this summer? Dad and I thought you were old enough to take the Greyhound to Opp, as long as you don't have to make too many changes en-route."

When she picked me off the floor I replied, "Are you kidding me? Shoot, I'd love to go, so when can I leave? Will Granny pick me up? What's the story?"

"I'll get the scoop from Greyhound and check with Granny to make sure you are picked up regardless of where the bus stops. You leave this Saturday, right after school lets out for the summer. I know you can't wait to see Rego, Aunt Evelyn, Uncle Johnny, Daddy Dean, and Granny. The sooner you leave the more time you'll have in Opp."

My heart was literally in my throat and I couldn't believe my own ears. For Mom and Dad to grant this much freedom had to say one of two things, or both. They trusted me enough to allow this solo journey, or they wanted to get me the hell out of Bethesda, as soon as possible. Can't for the life of me understand why they didn't just fly me down to Montgomery, except for the fact that mom was terrified of flying. I had my bags packed in about fifteen minutes after hearing this marvelous, too good to be true, proposition. I packed my suitcase, unpacked it, and re-packed it, again and again. Got all of my comics ready to go. Made sure I had my Levi's, tee shirts, tennis shoes and BVD's. And, a toothbrush. Didn't need a hairbrush . . . only had a crew cut. I'd wait until I reached Opp, before buying what would become my basic wardrobe for three months - a bathing suit.

Couldn't sleep that night and I didn't put away much in the way of breakfast because my stomach was nervous. The big day wouldn't be here for another twenty-four hours, so there was still a lot of time to contemplate the adventure of my measly lifetime.

The journey through the southern countryside and the small towns in Dixie that eventually lead to Opp, my favorite place in the whole world. Was I going to miss my so-called friend Chuck, and the rest of the gang from school? I began counting the hours until mom drove me down to buy the ticket. Apprehensive? Yes! Nervous? No. Excited? To the maximum! Mom made sure that I looked presentable in some new clothes she bought just for the trip because, as always, we didn't want the general public to infer Panky Miller was ill bred.

"Panky, I'll be warming up the Buick so get your bags and I'll see you in the car. Hurry it up. Jerry is in the backyard so why don't you go and say good-bye to him. He'll miss you so much this summer."

My dog, Jerry, a wire-haired fox terrier, was the apple of my eye. My parents bought him from a kennel in Virginia Beach, VA when I was in the first grade. Jerry was, undoubtedly, my very best friend, always doing his own thing, in his shy way. I was going to miss him but we were always used to going our separate ways. Unfortunately, I wasn't aware at this time that this would be our last few minutes together, because Jerry would meet his demise in the heavy traffic on Georgetown Road during the next couple of weeks. I didn't hear about his death until I returned from Opp, because my folks didn't think I could handle the news while on vacation. When I heard the news I must have cried for days because my best friend had left me, forever. I don't have a vivid recollection of Jerry the last time we were together.

"Mom, how much money will I have on the bus? And, how long is the trip? Will I be spending the night on board the Greyhound?"

"I'll give you twenty dollars for food and emergencies. Don't spend it all at your first stop or it'll be a mighty long and hungry trip for you, son. A word of advice. Try not to eat anything fishy or greasy so it won't upset your stomach, and you can call me collect on the phone it you have an emergency. Just ask the driver to help you. I'll call Granny with the route number, and the time it will arrive so you won't have to worry."

Can you imagine how I felt walking into the main Greyhound terminal, downtown Washington, D.C., in 1954? It was one scary experience. If you took every conceivable form of mankind imaginable they would eventually stroll into a bus station: Fat, thin, black, brown, white, rich, poor, well-groomed, slobs, fashionable, perfumes, body odor, sober, drunk, young and old. All walks of life from every corner of the globe. Everything I had been taught about sociology and geography was being put to the test today. Here I stood, lily white, 13 years old, innocent, very, very Catholic, the original preppie, as the ticket master asked, "Where are you headed, young man? "

I replied, "Opp, Alabama, sir, to see my grandparents and cousins for the summer."

"Here's your ticket and your mother can escort you out onto the bus ramp heading for Atlanta."

At last, the final few minutes, as we headed towards the gate where the ominous transports were parked.

"Sir, are you the driver of this bus?"

"Yes ma'am, would you like for me to keep an eye on this young man during the trip? He can sit here right behind me so we can talk, and he'll be just fine. I do this everyday and most folks seem to have a real good time on my trips. What's your name, son?"

"Panky Miller, and I'm heading for Opp, Alabama. Does this bus go that far?"

"No, we go as far as Atlanta. Then you'll have to change busses to Trailways, and maybe change again there, in Montgomery. I'll check your bag and you can put your carry-on with your magazines in the overhead rack. We'll be leaving in just a few minutes."

Ten minutes to say good-bye and to contemplate this excursion across America. What a rush I was getting from all this excitement. It was as if I had broken the tie that binds and had reached freedom at last. Let's get this bus on the road. After hugs and kisses from Mom I boarded the blue-white turkey, otherwise known as the Greyhound, and sank into my oversized, fully-adjustable, reclining, seat that was situated directly behind the driver. He looked sharp in his Greyhound uniform, was very polite, about forty years old, and from the northeast. No southern accent was detected so I assumed he was from this area. As he closed the big swinging front door I waved good-bye to mom for the last time and we rolled out of the parking lot on our journey. What a view. High up of the streets, over the tops of the cars, you could see things as never before. Nothing to block your vision. And, the air conditioning was fabulous. We didn't have the luxury of this amenity in either house or car, so this cool air was a real treat for me.

Unless you have traveled by bus you most likely have never really seen the people or the country, as you should. Can't watch all of those people and scenery if you driving - too much concentration on keeping the car on the road. And flying removes you completely from the realism of travel. The bus however provides you with the opportunity to really witness and experience travel at its best. Travel with a capital "T". Some folks say that travel by air shrinks the time when it, in fact, really shrinks the people. When you fly you do not have the opportunity to learn about the various cultures, the languages, the dialects, the smells, and the sounds. And, the changing of the clouds, the temperature, the humidity, all of those things that alert our senses to new experiences. So, flying really shrinks people rather than time because we diminish our ability to expand our horizons. Talk about the sights. Here we were passing the streetcars, the fabulous monuments and government buildings, the Little Tavern cafes that I frequented everyday after school, the beautiful tree-lined streets of Capitol Hill, and the other surrounding neighborhoods of Washington.

About this time when we were crossing into Virginia, the passengers on board began to relax and started conversations with those sitting in adjacent seats. This period in our history was during the era when black men and women were required by law to sit in the very back of the bus, and were not to fraternize with the white passengers. "To the back of the bus, boy," was heard much to often. This was, also, an era when smoking cigarettes was in vogue and almost everyone on board, save a few of the ladies, took out their Pall Malls, Camels, Picayunes, or whatever, and lit up. The smoke mixed with the air conditioning which was very unpleasant, and today it wouldn't be tolerated, but then again we're going back to the days when an individual's health was relative to other issues deemed more significant, like a good puff.

Let me tell you what you're missing if you travel by plane. All of the panoramas are opened not only to your vision but, also, to your imagination. When you travel past the various monuments, such as the one named in honor of George, or Abraham, or of the battle of Iwo Jima, your mind begins to play tricks. You begin to reenact the battles of Concord, the crossing of the Delaware, the Yankee victory at Appomattox, and the Japanese retreating from the beaches in the South Pacific. The streets whizzed by and soon we were out in the wide-open country bound for all points South, through Tyson's Corner, down towards Richmond, and Charlottesville VA; all of the names of the towns were familiar. . . Manassas, Mt. Vernon, Falls Church, Bull Run, Quantico. Counting telephone poles was another easy way to pass the time when you were tired of talking with your seatmate about school, or hobbies, or your family.

The thought of a nap was ridiculous. My nervous energy prevented such a luxury and so I was always looking out of the window just to wile away the time. Did you know that state laws require busses to stop at all railroad crossings? And, I mean every crossing, from Maine to Miami, from Norfolk to Newport Beach. Do you have any idea of how many railroad crossings exist in this land of ours? All you have to do is ride the bus cross-country to understand why the bus stops about every fifteen minutes during its journey, regardless of how long the route actually takes. For example, if your travel time is twenty-four hours you will stop at least ninety-six times **plus** the numerous times for passengers who are standing by the highway to board, **plus** the red lights, **plus** the scheduled stops. By the time you arrive at the final destination you have heard the air brakes of the bus at least a thousand times, and you will never forget for the rest of your life the smell of burning asbestos from those brakes for the rest of your life.

My excitement still was keeping the fatigue from setting in, and I wanted to stay awake for as long as possible so I wouldn't miss anything along the way. I always wondered who the folks were who waited to board, and where they were headed, whenever the bus stopped along the country roads. Some were obvious farm hands because of their odoriferous presence as they walked be me towards an empty seat. We're talking real body odor here, folks. It was as if a green cloud followed them down the isle. Whew! Our first scheduled stop was about to occur and we began to slow down in order to make the first turn-off onto the gravel in front of the country bus station.

"Folks, we're at Quantico, Virginia, and those debarking here can claim their bags inside the depot. For those continuing on to Atlanta, we'll be here for about thirty minutes."

Great, just enough time to look at the trinkets and to buy a snack because I was damn hungry by now. It was mid-afternoon and I was dying for a greasy hamburger and fries, ignoring what mom cautioned me about. I placed my order at the counter and then proceeded to wander over to the rack and eye the girlie magazines. Quickly, I came to the conclusion that it was best to move over to the comic book section to act as an ersatz cold shower. I had just enough time to gulp down my greasy cheese-burger and fries before reboarding the bus just to count what seemed like zillions of railroad crossings, and more stops. The driver began shifting through all of the gears, we were building speed, the speedometer was passing through fifty miles per hour and our high speed cruise began only to be interrupted by yet another one of those familiar circular yellow road signs with the black "X" indicating what hazard lay ahead. You guessed it. More railroad tracks, more delays, more frustration because I was in a hurry to get to Opp, so I could visit my cousins, grand-parents and friends.

It was getting to the point where all of these towns, counties and states were beginning to blur, and I no longer was aware of what State line we had crossed, whether we had left Virginia for North Carolina, South Carolina, or Tennessee. The humming of the tires along the blacktop, and the humming of the telephone poles that we sped by rang in my ears constantly. The country-side was typically eastern, southern and rural with the all too familiar Kudzu vine encompassing literally everything in its path. This invasive green ivy-like plant was developed to halt erosion in the southern soil but no one ever discovered how to restrict its growth. Eventually, the vine surely would cover the continent coast to coast, strangling everything along the way. I must admit, however, that the vine was beautiful as it crept up the red clay banks alongside the roads with its huge leaves glis-tening in the sunlight, and in the luminescence of moonlight. The deep green color provided a perfect contrast to the red clay soil, the whitewashed fences of the farms, and the asphalt shoul-ders of the highways. Mother nature, again, had done the right thing in pleasing the eye and the soul, albeit not the landowners who had to cope with a species gone haywire.

One of our scheduled stops was down in Taccoa, Georgia, which was the home of the world's strongest man. I think his name may have been Paul Anderson, and all of the magazines said he could lift a truck. That's right, an entire truck shown by the photographs in the papers, *Boy's Life,* and other magazines.

This was Taccoa's claim to fame and now when I hear of that town the first thing that comes to mind is Paul Anderson standing there with this truck on his back. As a 13 year old boy weighing a maximum of eighty pounds soaking wet, I was duly impressed by anyone who could lift a truck. So much for Taccoa, and it was time to move on down the road. Not too many more miles but countless telephone poles and railroad crossings until we could stretch our legs for that fifteen or twenty minutes at a whack.

"You are now entering the City of Atlanta," so read the sign as we zipped down the highway, and my pulse raced to unhealthy heights. One would have thought that this was the end of the line for me but far from it because we had several more hours until we arrived in Montgomery. Then, I suppose another bus change to Opp. Nonetheless, I was anxious to debark this thing we called home for the past twenty-four hours, and to stretch our legs. The Atlanta depot would be a welcome sight and, boy, was I looking forward to a good, hot meal, with the emphasis on good, not necessarily hot. The dining experiences over the past day and night left much to be desired and I'd rather not go into the details about how horrible most of the food tasted at those various depots stretching from Washington, down to Atlanta. Suffice it to say that the food was crummy. As we wound through the street approaching downtown Atlanta, we saw the magnificent buildings, the lovely antebellum houses, and the flowering dogwood trees. Atlanta was larger in both population and geography than Washington, and had the reputation of equal sophistication. I had relatives who lived in nearby Decatur. My paternal aunt and uncle, Uncle Bill and Aunt Jo, and my two cousins, Billy and Tommy, lived there but it never crossed my mind to inform them of my arrival so that we could possibly visit for a few hours. Heck, it was too late so I'd just look around in the shops, and take a walk down the street to Rich's Department Store, the biggest and best in the South.

Thank goodness the restaurant in the bus station had good southern food. I must have devoured five pieces of delicious fried chicken, with side orders of field peas, mashed potatoes, cornbread, tomatoes sliced with onions soaked in vinegar, and other foods that I missed for nine months of the year. I located the corner where the curios, magazines, and candy were sold. Why is it that every town has these satin pillowcases depicting local heroes, monuments or natural wonders? On top of that someone had the audacity to add gold fringe along the borders. We're talking ugly and I can't imagine anyone who would buy these souvenirs, but people do or they wouldn't still be in business. And the ceramic teepees which have Atlanta, or Stone Mountain, or the Cyclorama painted on the exterior. What in the hell does Atlanta have to do with a ceramic Indian teepee, I ask you? All across America these souvenirs were for sale and I have yet to see anyone buy a single one. A mystery of the cosmos, indeed. Of course, I could always buy a thimble for Granny which was made of some cheap metal alloy with some building, like the capitol dome, embossed on the circumference. Lordy, there wasn't one single thing left to buy for my grandmother. Only one thing left was a crummy postcard that she could keep as a memoir.

Back on the bus and on our way to Montgomery, "The Cradle of the Confederacy." Time enroute . . . four and one-half hours, estimated, as we bade farewell to Atlanta, and the magnificent countryside was, once again, our own personal panorama. Towns like Fayetteville, Newnan, Pine Mountain, La Grange, Opelika, Auburn, Tuskegee, were our scheduled stops as the topography went from flat to hilly to small mountains back to the plains of Alabama. Every small hamlet, every railroad crossing, every bus depot, every country store, every town water tank, every shanty and farmhouse had its own personal signature, albeit southern in character. And, more and more humming down that blacktop passing the endless parallel lines of telephone poles converging into a point over the horizon. Field after field of cotton waiting to be picked juxtaposed to tall yellow corn burning in the heat of the southern sun, rows of soybeans that eventually became an ingredient in almost everything we consumed or applied to our bodies. And, peanuts, my heavens, peanuts that were the staple of America. We ate them roasted, creamed into butter, boiled and ground. My favorite of all the crops grown in this region, however, was sugarcane. I can't think of a more delicious sweet than sucking the sugar right from the stalk while spitting the husks onto the ground. Messy and uncouth, but damn good.

Shortly after three o'clock we arrived at the Montgomery depot and just in time to catch the last Trailways bus heading South towards the Gulf of Mexico, and Opp, my destination. I grabbed my bags and made certain that the bus I was boarding was the right one and would eventually arrive in Opp.

"Sir, is this the bus to Opp?"

The driver said, "Sure is, sonny, and you're not a minute too soon. That bus from Atlanta almost made you late enough to miss this bus, which means you'd have to catch another one tomorrow."

Butterflies hit my stomach like you can't imagine! What would have I done if I'd missed that bus to Opp? Spend the night on a bench in the depot? Walk the streets of Montgomery, all night long and cook breakfast with the hoboes in the train yard? At this point I was extremely thankful that we were still able to make that bus. My state of panic was finally subsiding. Throughout this portion of my trip I had the luxury of sitting alone and not having to worry about making conversation with my fellow travelers for hours upon end. This situation was about to change because the bus was going to have a full contingency of passengers and the seat adjacent to mine was one of the few still vacant. One of the last passengers to board was a man, probably in his late twenties, red hair, red freckles, weathered skin, crows feet 'round his eyes, a cowboy-style plaid shirt, Levis, boots . . .and only one eye. Only one eye! Where most everyone had two eyes, he had just one eye and the other socket was missing an eyeball! Naturally, he headed straight for me and asked, "This seat taken, boy?"

I tried my damndest not to stare, to regain my composure, and to reply, unemotionally, "No sir, it's all yours."

He threw his duffel bag in the top overhead rack, sat down and, after a few minutes, asked where I was from and where I was headed. My parents always taught me it was impolite to stare at people but, in this case, I couldn't help it. "I live in Bethesda, Maryland, just outside of Washington, and I'm heading down to Opp, to spend the summer with my relatives. This is my first bus trip alone and I've been traveling since yesterday morning. Where are you from, and where are you going?"

"I'm heading down to Florida, to work in the fields. My family has a farm and it's time for the harvest, so I'm going down to help 'em. I've been through Opp, many times on my way to Kinston, where I have kinfolk. Do you know where that is?"

"Sure do, and the man who bought my granddaddy's drugstore is from Kinston. I usually get to spend the summers with my grandparents and my cousins, but sometime we get transferred too far away for me to come visit. My daddy's a Naval officer, so we travel a lot. I really look forward to the times when I come down to Opp, so I can swim everyday, go to the matinees, and eat lots of great food cooked by Gladdy Mae, my granny's maid."

This was my life's story. Didn't want to talk about school, 'cause I hated school. Didn't want to talk about my friends 'cause they weren't really my true friends. All I really wanted to talk about was my dog, Jerry, and my summers with my real friends, Uncle Johnny, Aunt Evelyn, cousins Rego, Stevie and Carol, and Granny and Daddy Dean.

Two hours into the trip we both dozed off. Upon awakening, I could tell by the towns we passed and, as we turned at the junction with about eight or ten more miles left to go, I began to get fidgety. Couldn't site still for the life of me and I began to mildly hyperventilate. After traveling through five states for over twenty-four hours I was about as excited as a boy could be. We stopped at everyone of those cotton-picking railroad crossings, all stop lights, all stop signs, until those final few hundred yards that would bring us to the Opp depot.

I almost jumped out of the bus window when my neighbor with one eye said, "Panky, don't ever forget who you are and where you're from. You're a smart kid with a good education and you've got good kinfolk to take care of you. I know that my eye scares you, but it doesn't scare me, so try to remember how other people feel about themselves. It's not how a person looks that makes 'em good or bad. It is what's inside and in their hearts that makes them good, decent folk. You remember what I told you and you'll be all right down the road. Take care of yourself, boy."

I looked him straight in his good eye and replied, "I sure will and you do the same. Hope you can help your family down in Florida. I see my grandmother and cousins, so I'll see you later." I grabbed my bag and comics, and scurried down the steps as fast as I could into my grandmother's arms amidst the shouts from Rego that he could hardly wait to go the pool tomorrow.

Nearly thirty hours, thousand of railroad crossings, millions of telephone poles, acres of kudzu vine, countless greasy hamburgers and Cokes, incessant humming of the bus tires and the telephone poles, numerous stops in the country for passengers, two bus changes, smelly cigarette smoke mixed with the air conditioning, several very nice and professional bus drivers, and honest man with more vision from his one eye that most people have with two, I was home at last.

To be continued in BOOK TWO.

113